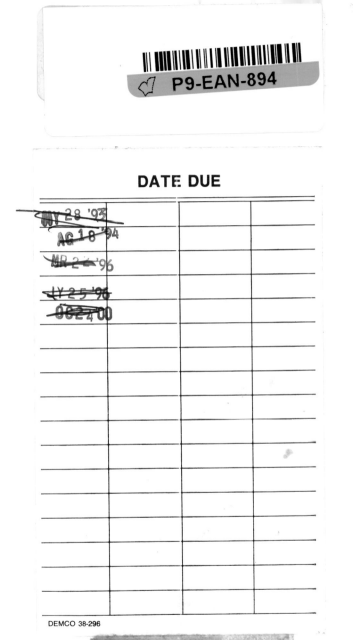

CAREGIVING

Also by E. Jane Mall

Kitty, My Rib
Beyond the Rummage Sale
Abingdon Manual of Installation Services
A Mother's Gifts
How to Become Wealthy Publishing a Newsletter
*And God Created Wrinkles

*Also published by Ballantine Books

CAREGIVING

How to Care for

Your Elderly Mother

and Stay Sane

E. JANE MALL

A Ballantine/Epiphany Book

Ballantine Books · New York

A Ballantine/Epiphany Book
Published by Ballantine Books
Copyright © 1990 by E. Jane Mall

Library of Congress Cataloging-in-Publication Data

Mall, E. Jane, 1920–
Caregiving : how to care for your elderly mother and stay sane /
E. Jane Mall.—1st ed.
p. cm.
"A Ballantine/Epiphany book."
Includes bibliographical references.
ISBN 0-345-36460-0
1. Parents, Aged—Care—United States. 2. Aged women—Care—
—United States. 3. Mothers and daughters—United States.
4. Caregivers—United States—Psychology. I. Title.
HQ1063.6.M35   1990
649.8—dc20   89-91521
CIP

Design by Holly Johnson

Manufactured in the United States of America

First Edition: August 1990

10 9 8 7 6 5 4 3 2 1

Dedicated to Pat and Ozzie Mall, who are loving, caring
caregivers to their two mothers and who helped me
so much in the writing of this book.
And also dedicated to my beautiful, loving
caregiving daughter, Heide.
And to Toni Simmons, the most helpful and
supportive editor I have ever known.

A stream that always flows in one direction may be likened to an elderly parent, whose lifestyle and habits are set and cannot be changed. We need to work with the stream and channel the flow slowly into new outlets.

—PATT ENSING, A CAREGIVER
ALLENDALE, MICHIGAN

CONTENTS

I will turn all my mountains into roads,
and my highways will be raised up.

—ISAIAH 49:11

FOREWORD

This book is addressed to caregivers: women who have been called members of "the sandwich generation." In age you fall all the way between forty and sixty; sometimes with children still at home, or in college; some of you have grand-children; some are coping with the onslaught of menopause. To you falls the responsibility of caring for your elderly mothers and mothers-in-law. Some men are caregivers also, but the majority are women. Many aspects of caregiving are the same for men and women, but I decided to focus on the special relationship between daughter and aging mother.

About 30 percent of the women caregivers work full-time outside the home and have children under eighteen. They spend approximately 10 hours a week in caregiving. That adds up to 40 hours a month, 480 hours a year. The older your mother gets, the more hours you spend on her caregiving.

You are all pioneers. Never before have people lived long enough for caregiving to become a problem. In fact, caring for elderly parents is fast becoming a major cause of stress in American families. As if you needed yet another cause for stress!

What exactly is caregiving? It's difficult to define because it embraces so much, physically and emotionally. It is giving care to a person who needs to be cared for in certain areas. One person's caregiving may include a lot of driving here and there, shopping, cleaning, and so forth. Another's may consist of a daily phone call. However, most caregiving consists of nurturing: a phone call once a day, shopping once a week, letting your mother know that you love her and that you're there for her when she needs you. Later on, when your mother gets really old, more caregiving may be required. Maybe not. I know of many women in their eighties and nineties who live alone and require very little caregiving. What is needed most is your expression of love toward your mother, your understanding of what aging is doing to her. It's letting her know that she is still important to you and cherished by you. Your mother's old age goes on for a long time, and there are things you can do to help make those years happy and peaceful. There are things your mother can and should do, too, but this book is directed to you, the caregiver. (For books your mother can read, see Resources.)

Some years back I was a caregiver but I didn't have the title. In fact twenty-odd years ago I thought of a caregiver as someone who worked on lawns. Or in institutions. Today caregivers of elderly mothers comprise a very large segment of the population.

When I was a caregiver, it was easy because it didn't last very long. My mom moved in with my husband and me when she was sixty-four. After my husband died, she lived with me and my children until she died at the age of sixty-nine. It was a short time in my life and I didn't plan for it or agonize over the mechanics of it. My mother was simply integrated into my family for a few years.

The scene has changed dramatically since my mother died in 1966. More and more people are living longer and longer, and the caregiving role has become, or will become, a part of nearly everyone's life. At one time if you got close to one hundred, you could almost be sure of being invited as a guest on the Johnny Carson show. Now it is being predicted for the nineties that we will have around one million centenarians.

My mother-in-law is still active at the age of ninety-four, lives alone, and is in need of some caregiving. This falls to her only remaining son and his wife. They also care for the wife's widowed mother. They have been in it for the long haul and have had to do some planning and changing of plans over the years. This seems to be fairly typical for the majority of caregivers.

Caregivers are motivated by love. You want to take care of your mother. You love her and feel that it's your duty. If there is some guilt involved, or too much of a sense of duty, you either aren't aware of it or you repress it. After all, what choice do you have? You can't put your mother out on the street or just leave her alone to shift for herself. The trouble is, caregivers take on the role but too often are incapable of meeting all of the elderly parent's needs. They're not even sure what those needs are. This is virgin territory, and today's caregivers are asking many questions and seeking solutions.

This book is directed to the caregivers whose mothers are emotionally and physically stable. I realize that many caregivers are caring for elderly fathers rather than, or in addition to, mothers. Probably many of the caregiving techniques and duties are the same, but in this book I focus on the unique mother-daughter relationship.

Some caregivers have special problems with mothers

who have Alzheimer's disease or are crippled with arthritis or the aftermath of an accident. Some mothers become alcoholics or extreme "Poor Paulines." These require special knowledge and care. One couple, in their early sixties, was able to give the man's eighty-year-old mother minimal care until she developed diabetes and had to give herself insulin shots. When they discovered that she was waking several times in the night and each time administering a shot, she had to be moved to a nursing home.

A parent with Alzheimer's is probably better off in a home with professional, round-the-clock care. I know a woman whose father suffered from Alzheimer's. She was determined to care for her dear dad until one day a neighbor phoned: "Your dad is strolling down the highway in traffic!" The next afternoon the same neighbor called. "Your dad climbed a tree in our yard. He's way up in a top branch and I don't think he can get down." For his own safety he had to be put into a home. It can be heartrending to put a parent in a nursing home, but common sense must prevail. Most communities have support groups for those with relatives who have Alzheimer's.

The magic word for successful caregiving is planning—long before you're faced with a crisis or with having to "do something about Mom." One woman wrote to me: "I am not a note-taking, list-making kind of person. I plan it all in my head, talk it over with my mother, and we forge ahead." However you do your planning, just be sure you do it. It won't all turn out exactly as you plan, but no planning at all can be disastrous. It's a matter of considering what might happen and what you will be able to do about it. This planning includes your mother's input and exploration on your part of the options, what help is available, and how you can stay sane through it all. *Caregiving* will guide you as you plan.

Today's caregiver will probably be taking on a ten-to-twenty-year commitment. It's imperative that you know what you're doing and why, and that you're able to care for your mother in the best possible way. You could muddle through and your mother would survive, but what about you? These last years of your mother's life should be pleasant, filled with love and sweet memories for you in the years ahead. For the most part you know how to do the required physical things, such as shopping and cleaning. The emotional and psychological aspects of caregiving must be learned so that you don't get "used up" during your caregiving years. It is my hope that this book will help.

I am sixty-nine years old and my daughter, Heide, is my primary caregiver. I have been on both sides of the fence and have seen firsthand that caregivers can use some direction. You are performing a selfless act of love and you are worthy of all the help you can get.

I have included a quiz (page 38) to determine how grown up you are, particularly in your relationship with your mother; another (page 22) to dispel some of the myths about old age. There is a listing of the elderly woman's needs and also the needs of the caregiver. There is a questionnaire to be completed by both you and your mother (page 155) to determine where you stand emotionally, how you differ, how you're alike; your honest responses will give both of you a deeper understanding of your roles.

What about having your mother live with you? In spite of the exceptions, having your mother live with you is nearly always the worst possible choice. Very seldom does the elderly parent want to move in with a son or daughter.

The invitation is usually offered out of a sense of guilt or duty. Once your mother is in your home, it's extremely difficult to change circumstances. Your mother stays, resented by you, gradually losing her independence, and no one is happy. One woman wrote to me, "My mom moved in with us. It didn't work, so she moved out. Now we're happy again." Rarely is it as simple as that. In case it becomes necessary for your mother to live with you, I have included a chapter on how to cope and make the best of it for all concerned.

Several pages of resources conclude this book. There are listings of books to read, pamphlets on many aspects of aging and caregiving, and organizations to join. Many of these require only a postcard or phone call asking for a free item. Depending on your area of interest, many of these can be extremely helpful.

I would like to see a caregiver publish a newsletter. Some years back I started a newsletter for church secretaries. I began with no subscribers and in a few years had subscribers in every state and many in Canada. Someone else is publishing it now and it's still going strong and growing. I have watched others come and go and I believe I know the secret of success: Most important, I was a church secretary, so I knew what I was talking about, and the newsletter was a vehicle for sharing. Church secretaries shared their problems and triumphs. They asked each other questions. I had a "Trading Post" section so that they could correspond with each other. I believe caregivers would welcome a newsletter on this order. You can work at home and your mother can help with the mailings. My publication eventually led to church-secretary workshops and seminars all over the country. Can someone envision this for caregivers?

I have so much admiration for you pioneer caregivers.

You are acting out of love, which reduces the burden, but it's not easy to choreograph your life to please so many and still have something left for yourself. My prayer is that this book will help.

SECTION I

Getting Ready

Where there is no vision,
the people perish.

PROVERBS 29:18a

CHAPTER 1

Planning Ahead

Old age is not a sickness that may strike suddenly. To a great extent you can prepare yourself for it. As your mother's caregiver, it's essential that you plan, along with your mother, as early as possible, for the caregiving years. Your mother will grow old and older, whether or not you do any planning, but without anticipating what the years will bring, you will be a most inadequate caregiver.

My mother never told me about menstruation. It happened on a Sunday night and I was appalled, frightened, and ashamed. I said nothing about it and wore two pairs of panties to school the next morning. Before the first class was over, I was sent home, more embarrassed than I had ever been in my life.

My mother said, "Well, you have come sick. It will happen once a month." She gave me two towels, a belt, and safety pins. Sick! Instantly I felt terrible and spent the rest of the day in bed. My only consolation was that it wasn't my fault.

It's easy to see how some advance preparation would have made this event less traumatic. (It's also too bad that my mother thought of it as "coming sick" but I corrected that with my daughters.)

A big reason for planning is that, as pioneers, you are setting the stage, making the rules for future generations of caregivers. Eliminate the errors, dispel the myths, and set it up right for your daughters.

My children are very good to me. We have a great give-and-take relationship, we don't get in each other's way, and we love each other.

When he is with me, my son does most of the cooking. This works fine, because he loves to cook and I hate it. The fact that I load the dishwasher and clean up after him suits him very well.

My daughter takes me grocery shopping once a week. After our excursion we always go someplace for lunch and I pick up the check.

One time I decided to find out how it would be if I couldn't do my share. Believe me, my eyes were opened. I became "ill" with a vague, rather mysterious stomach ailment. I felt weak, I had trouble sleeping, and I simply wasn't up to doing much of anything.

The kitchen and dishes stayed dirty. "I tried," I told my son, "but I couldn't finish the job. I felt so weak I had to lie down." Carlton hung in for an alarmingly long time but finally had to give in and load the dishwasher.

I absolutely couldn't manage the weekly shopping trips or going out for lunch. I asked my daughter, "Would you mind picking up a few things for me?" and I hauled out my weekly shopping list.

It didn't take long before I sensed hostility and even disgust. This wasn't the mom they knew. I wasn't fun any-more, and I was becoming dependent on them. They were puzzled, and not especially kind. ("Why don't you go to a doctor and get whatever it is fixed?") I can't begin to imagine how long they would have endured this without becoming bitter. How much longer would our once happy relationship have lasted?

Before you start calling my kids rotten, let me tell you something. They reacted in a normal way. Let's face it, we are all basically quite selfish. We are not happy when things get uncomfortable for us. If I had been truly ill and needed their help over a long period of time, I'm sure they would have come through for me.

It was a tough lesson, but I had to face the truth. This very thing will happen, to some degree, if I live long enough.

It frightens me. Not the children's attitude—sure they would have rallied in time—but the thought of losing my independence scares me. Also, I can't stand the thought of my children viewing me as a burden. All old women I have talked to share these same feelings.

Oh, I saw the need for planning ahead, of talking about the possibilities, how they feel about my aging and how I feel. What they will do and what I will do. How we will be able to manage and keep our relationship a good one. We can, I know, if we plan ahead together.

The first step is simple: Talk to your mother. I know, this sounds too easy, but most caregivers don't broach the topic, and therein lie most of the problems. I suppose the reason is that it forces you to admit that your mother is getting old. And gets her to admit it. It also brings up the issue that it happens to everyone, even you, and you would rather not think about that. Your mother doesn't particularly care to talk about the future either, so asking her to discuss what should be done in a crisis involving her advancing age seems almost cruel. You have to force yourself to do it. Say, "Mom, we have a long time ahead of us. I want this time to be the best it can be for both of us." Be gentle and understanding. "Right now you seem so young to me, Mom, but maybe we should look ahead and do some planning together." Perhaps you know of some elderly women who are having a very hard time of it partially because they, and their caregiving daughters, were caught off guard. Tell your mother that you don't want her to experience a similar predicament.

When my children were young, we moved several times, and in each new house we conducted a fire drill. "If there is a fire in the kitchen, we will . . . ," and so on. We never had a fire, but we were prepared. I could have had the best plan in the world, but if the children and I hadn't planned it together and gone through the motions together, it wouldn't have been any help when fire broke out.

The earlier you start planning and talking with your mother, the better. I am not suggesting one afternoon of discussion, of getting it out of the way and then forgetting it. These planning talks must be ongoing, like aging itself.

"Remember, Mom, you said that you want to be cremated. Do you still feel that way or have you changed your mind?" One caregiver put off these planning discussions because it was so sad to be talking to her beloved mother about death. Then her mother had a stroke and was unable to communicate with her in any way. She cared for her mother the best she could, but she had no idea of how she felt. She imagined that she saw pain in her mother's eyes because of some of the things she did, but she couldn't be sure.

Imagine the worst and get busy. Ask your mother where she would want to live if she couldn't manage on her own. How does she feel about a nursing home? Has she written a will?

If possible, all family members, including spouses and

grandchildren, should be in on this planning, but if it's not possible, let the absent members know what the plans are and how you intend to execute them. Now is the time to request input and assistance from other family members. Later, if your mother makes any significant changes, all family members should be told about them.

Everyone should understand what the plans involve. Everyone should be willing to make some kind of a commitment. If they're not, don't let it burden you. You have told them what the plans are, you have requested a commitment, and that's all you have to do. You can still keep that member informed as to what's going on in Mom's life, and maybe one day a commitment of some kind will be forthcoming. If not, it's not your problem.

You are the principal caregiver, so the everyday details are left to you and your mother. How you handle these is your business, and you are accountable to no one but each other. Make that clear to everyone. You can't have a sister telling you, "I think you should take Mom to the early church service. That was always her favorite time to go," or a brother saying, "Take her out to a movie now and then." These details are none of their business.

A brother who lives nearby but is not involved in the everyday caregiving can make a commitment. He can take Mom out to dinner once a month, call her on a regular basis, maybe now and then bring his friends over to meet his mother. He can pledge an amount of money if it's needed.

Get everyone in on the act. Grandchildren can make commitments too. A boy or girl who drives can assume some of their grandmother's trips to the doctor, dentist, and so on; they can do her yard work, help clean house, go to her home and talk to her, sometimes bring their friends. Young people can be thoughtless, but if you suggest some of the things they can do for their grandmother, and how much what they do will be appreciated, the chances are the kids will surprise you. Their participation is necessary for several reasons: Your mother will know that her whole family loves her, cares about her, and is involved in the caregiving role. This is about the best gift you can give her. Then you, as the principal caregiver, won't have to experience the martyr syndrome. "I do so much for Mom and they do nothing!" And when your mother dies and her will reveals equal distribution of her assets, you won't feel bitter and resentful. Your brothers and sisters won't be able to pop on the scene one day and say, "Oh, Mom, if I had known she was doing this, I would have stopped her." Or, "If you had only told me about this, I would have helped."

There is another vital aspect for you to consider during this planning stage. You have to decide how your actions as caregiver will affect other areas of your life.

For example, you may be perfectly willing to take your mother to her bingo games every Monday night. However, that's your husband's bowling night, and he likes you to go with him, even though you're not on the team. Make other arrangements for your mother to get to her bingo game: a car-pool arrangement with other bingo players, a lift from your son, or a taxi. The time may come when you will have to sacrifice some time with your husband and family in order to care for your mother. Wait until it's necessary. (This is discussed more fully in later chapters.)

If you work outside the home, planning ahead is the only way you'll keep your sanity. You have a husband, perhaps children at home, a house, shopping for various items, a social life, plus a mother who needs you for certain things. This involves quite a balancing act and you shouldn't shortchange yourself. Whether you're working because you need the money or because it's a career you enjoy, it's meaningful to you. You can't take time off whenever you feel like it; you can't go to work so tired you can't think straight. You have to figure out your priorities and let everyone concerned know what they are.

Jessie worked at a full-time job and cared very well for her husband and one sixteen-year-old son still at home. She was also her mother's caregiver. Jessie and her husband were on a bowling team that bowled twice a week; they went out to dinner with friends every Friday. Her son needed help during the week with a reading program. Jessie's mother called every evening and also called her at work nearly every day. Jessie loved her job and had worked hard to advance to the position she held. She had been living a very full, busy life, and this was fine until she took on the extra duties and responsibilities of caregiver to her mother. Now her Saturday mornings were consumed with taking her mother grocery shopping and on Sundays she attended church with her mother. She felt very guilty because her mother was alone so much of the time. She began having severe head aches and what she called a "nervous stomach."

After Jessie had canceled another bowling date, her husband said, "You have got to quit that damned job!" and Jessie knew that her marriage was on the brink of trouble.

The problem was, she was allowing herself to be used up, scattered in too many directions, and deriving little satisfaction from any of it. What Jessie finally did was smart. She sat down with her husband and together they listed priorities, drafted a workable schedule, enlisted the help of their son and some people at church, and then both Jessie and her husband talked it over with Jessie's mother. Their planning worked fine for Jessie and everyone concerned.

During the planning stage, list your mother's needs.

(Don't forget, these will almost certainly change as the years go by.) Before you agree to anything, ask yourself, "If I do this, how will it affect my marriage/children/job/social life, and so on?"

If you don't set priorities and consider everyone right from the start, both you and your mother will probably regret it.

Write down all the factors and be sure everyone concerned has copies of everything. By doing this early on, you can avoid misunderstandings and resentment. The list does not have to include details such as "I drive Mom to church every Sunday."

Your first written report, with copies sent to your siblings, might look like this:

• Mom's monthly income is adequate to cover her expenses with a little money left over each month. (If it's all right with your mother, you can quote actual figures.)

• Mom has decided to stay where she is for the time being. If a move is indicated later on, you will be notified.

• Mom's health is fine. (You could quote the latest medical report.)

• Mom does not want, under any circumstances, to go to a nursing home. Her desire may or may not become negotiable.

• I have safety-proofed Mom's home as much as possible in order to avoid accidents. (Give details if you want to.)

• Mom has written a Living Will; has given me durable power of attorney; has named me executor of her will; has expressed a desire in writing to be cremated. (Instead, perhaps list the details of her funeral plans.)

• In conclusion, Mom is healthy, reasonably content and financially okay. Loneliness appears to be her biggest complaint. More frequent phone calls and letters from all of you would help.

Date and sign this document and send copies, not only to your siblings but to other close relatives as well.

In this planning section I have tried to cover the essentials needed to plan for your caregiving years. In the next chapters we will deal with emotions and expectations and get down to business with specifics.

CHAPTER 2

False Tales About Aging

How old is old? The answer to this question has changed dramatically in recent years. Today caregivers are of the age that, not long ago, was considered elderly. I read about an eighty-two-year-old woman putting her ninety-eight-year-old mother into a nursing home because she was getting too old to care for her. And a fifty-five-year-old woman, dying of cancer, whose greatest concern was that there was no one to take care of her mother.

It's absolutely necessary that the caregivers understand the aging process. No longer can we dismiss everything that happens by saying, "Oh, well. She's old. It's to be expected."

Everyone ages differently. Some accept it and go with the flow. Others fight it to the point of absurdity. Of course, health, finances, and any number of other circumstances have an effect. An elderly woman who lives with the constant pain of arthritis or with the fear of another heart attack is going to require special caregiving. Some aging women find loneliness an almost intolerable burden, while others keep busy and interested in many things. The caregiver will have to study her own mother to decide how she is aging and what she needs.

The *Los Angeles Times* Poll conducted a nationwide survey that determined that old age is not as bad as many Americans have come to fear. Most elderly people will agree with that.

Most of the findings of the survey are right on target: they say that nearly two-thirds of Americans over sixty-five are pleased with their personal lives. Most older people are keeping busy doing the things they didn't have time for before retirement.

The survey reveals that older people are less concerned about money, less likely to be lonely or depressed, and less fearful of disease and death. I believe it's true that old people, regardless of how much or how little money they have, don't worry about it. They are through struggling with mortgage payments and worries about how to pay for new furniture and children's clothes and school supplies. However, many old people are lonely. In fact, loneliness is a prevailing theme among elderly widows. They cope the best they can, because most have no choice, but loneliness colors their lives.

It is true that the fear of death fades with each advancing year. I believe that this is not a conscious act, but a marvelous thing that simply happens.

The survey indicated that the older people are, the younger they feel. In my opinion this is hogwash. It is probably a form of denial. The reality is, older people can't do many of the things they could do when they were young. The delightful thing is they don't particularly want to. Anyway, why compare the young with the old? They are two separate stages of life and each has its own pains and joys and triumphs and limitations.

The caregiver should try to explode a few myths about old age:

• *Myth: Old people don't have any fun and don't want any.* A twenty-year-old's idea of fun isn't necessarily fun for an older person. Old people have fun in different ways. Having a cup of coffee with an old, dear friend is fun. Playing a game of poker for peanuts or buttons is fun, too, especially if it's played with the grandchildren. Many old people go on vacations alone and take cruises. They play bingo, swim, go horseback riding, play tennis and golf. Some are into mountain climbing, cross-country skiing, and boating. For some, romance and dating is still a part of their lives. Oh, yes, old people like to have fun.

• *Myth: Old people lose their memory.* My twenty-seven-year-old daughter forgets things too. It's funny. Both of us forget what we wanted at the store, but we can recall tiny details from the past. If we don't keep things percolating and don't use our minds, whether we're young or old, we're going to be forgetful. It doesn't have to do with age so much as with laziness or inactivity. Or else we were born a little on the stupid side and never could remember anything.

There is a joke going around about forgetfulness. I believe it illustrates how unimportant a matter it really is:

> An older couple was watching TV. The man started for the kitchen.
>
> Wife: "Where are you going?"
> Husband: "I'm going to the kitchen to get some ice cream."
> Wife: "Oh, that sounds good. Bring me some too."
> Husband: "Okay."
> Wife: "I want vanilla."
> Husband: "Okay."
> Wife: "And put some chocolate sauce on it."

Husband: "Okay."
Wife: "And a little whipped cream too."
Husband: "Okay."
Wife: "Sprinkle a few nuts on top."
Husband: "Okay."
The husband left the room and after a while returned and handed his wife a ham sandwich.
Wife: "Oh, you are so forgetful!"
Husband: "Why do you say that?"
Wife: "You forgot the mustard!"

I work crossword puzzles and I read a lot. Anyone can do these things regardless of age. The picture of the old woman searching for her glasses while they are perched on top of her head doesn't mean much. It could just as well be a young woman. As long as old people keep mentally active, their memories will be all right.

Some older people do suffer a loss of memory. Its importance depends on the degree of loss. One old woman, constantly forgetting where she put things, can be sort of cute. "Okay, let's all look for Mom's keys. She lost them again!" However, it can also be annoying and even dangerous. If your mother forgets to pay her rent and utility bills, for example, you will have to figure out a way either to pay them for her or to remind her each month. If her memory loss is so bad that every time she goes for a walk she forgets how to get home, or if she forgets to take her prescription medication, it can be a serious problem.

I have learned that I don't really forget things, I just have trouble recalling them from that computer in my head. I also use little tricks to help jog my memory. You could suggest some of these to your mother.

For example, if there is a certain chore she wants to do

the next day, such as defrosting the refrigerator or cleaning the oven, she can put a lamp or vase in the middle of the living room floor before going to bed. The next morning that lamp or vase will immediately remind her of what she wanted to do. Writing notes is helpful. Setting an alarm clock for a certain time. The ringing immediately reminds you that you have something to do. One woman has a bright red scarf, and when it's tied to something or draped over something, it reminds her of what she planned to do. Any tricks like these that work can be a big help and can boost self-esteem. They can also serve as a safety measure. For instance, if your mother writes a note to herself or sets the alarm clock every time she puts something on the stove or in the oven, she will reduce the possibility of a fire.

• *Myth: Old people lose their strength and become frail and helpless.* Sure, but we're talking real old-old here. Like close to one hundred. Most of the elderly are doing okay. They walk, exercise, take care of themselves, eat the right foods. They don't become frail and helpless for a long time. Don't baby your mother; she doesn't want or need that. Help her keep her strength.

I remember a day in the supermarket. The cashier was checking out my groceries and my daughter was bagging them. I stood between them, waiting to write a check. The cashier said, over my head, to my daughter, "Heide, does she want both canned pears and fresh pears or did she make a mistake?"

Heide answered, "She wants both."

I was very angry but I said nothing. (Old ladies learn the art of patience.)

Then the cashier said, again over my head, "Does she want her groceries bagged in plastic or paper bags?"

Heide replied, "She likes the plastic."

That's when I blew my top. (Old people are patient, not brain-damaged.) "Listen, you two. I am here! Those are my groceries. Talk to me. Ask me what I want."

The astonished expressions on their faces almost made me laugh. "I'm so sorry, Mrs. Mall."

"Mama, I'm sorry!"

Two old ladies and one elderly man in line behind me applauded! Speaking out was the best thing I could have done. It was better than burying my hurt feelings, muttering something about old-age discrimination, and carrying that resentment around. Remember, your mother can think and speak for herself.

There are exceptions. Some mothers are nearly crippled with arthritis, or suffer acute hearing loss, or have cataracts. They need more care and understanding than the active, healthy elderly, but their minds are still in good working order.

• *Myth: Old people are preoccupied with death.* No way, José! It's a sobering fact that they are probably closer to death than you are, that they have all that mileage behind them and not much ahead. Of course. That's the way it is by ordination of God, and they accept it. They don't dwell on it. There will be times when death looms very large. When your mother's friends and relatives die, one by one, the fact of her own impending death is brought to the forefront. Be sympathetic and understanding during these times. Let your mother talk about her friends and relatives. "I remember Aunt Mary so well, Mom. She was such a loving person." Traveling with her in memory can be a great comfort to your mother.

When I was young, I used to think there was an aura of death around old people. I see now how foolish I was. Old people have seen too many die before they ever got old.

Starving children, young people who overdosed on drugs or raced a car to destruction. They know, and you should know, that death is no respecter of persons.

• *Myth: Old people are set in their ways.* Did it ever occur to you that they are set in their ways because they have figured out what's best and what they like? They're not still searching and groping for a life-style or career. They have wisely learned to accept some things the way they are.

Your mother is home alone a good deal of the time. She takes morning walks, cleans house if she feels like it. She writes letters, watches Oprah, reads books. She sews. She's content. Okay, so she does certain things at certain times in certain ways. So what? She's comfortable with her routine, she knows what works for her, and it shouldn't bother you. What's so terrible about set ways? If a friend calls and invites your mother to go out for lunch or for a drive, she goes. Sometimes, if no one invites her anywhere for a long time, she goes out on her own. Let her do these things, admire her for living her life the way she wants to live it. The myth about old people being set in their ways is sort of true, but not entirely. Sort of, because they are, but in some areas it's because they like it the way it is.

Those are some of the myths that need to be erased. Today's old people are nothing like those of yesteryear. Old people know about the body's immune system and the ways in which the mind can keep the body healthy. Many practice positive thinking, have a strong faith, and feel more creative in old age than they ever did all the years they worked for a paycheck.

Some old people have surrendered to the onslaughts of aging, and your mother may be one of them. She may complain, talk about how lonely she is, how she has nothing to do, how no one cares about her. In other words she may take a completely negative attitude toward her aging. You can help by refusing to indulge her. Tell her you don't believe all the old myths and horror stories about aging. You can't make her read or take a walk or call a friend. You can't be with her all the time to ease her loneliness. Instead suggest books you think she will enjoy, try to get her interested in needlework or a huge jigsaw puzzle or baking cookies for the grandchildren. Call her every day. If nothing works, she will have to wallow in her own misery, believing the myth that old age is a terrible time.

After the publication of my book *And God Created Wrinkles*, I received hundreds of letters. Nearly every one was positive, uplifting, and told stories of what old people across the country are doing with their lives. As I read those letters, I cried, I laughed, and I put away forever the myth that old people are set in their ways, unhappy, and inflexible.

Another myth is that old people aren't happy unless they are near at least one of their children, especially during holidays. Some modern mothers don't feel this way at all. I recall one mother moaning because her kids always insisted on the whole clan getting together for Thanksgiving. She wanted to spend that day with a group of widows her age. There was a terrible conflict over this and there shouldn't have been. Your mother has the right to do as she pleases.

My son chose to spend one Thanksgiving with his girlfriend and her family rather than with us. Let me tell you, my feelings were hurt, but I didn't let him know. Only a rotten mom would make her kid suffer for such a thing. You can be a rotten kid if you try to lay a guilt trip on your mother for something like this.

The young seem to assume that life must be terrible for

old people. Their assumption is rooted in plain ignorance. If you are a caregiver, it will be smart of you to learn the truth.

For instance, I keep discovering little advantages in growing old. Here's one:

When I was young so many things were somehow my fault. "Jane, your skin looks terrible! You've been eating fried foods, haven't you? Or was it chocolate?"

"You have another headache? Okay, what have you been worrying about now?"

"It's only eight in the evening and you're tired? I guess you have been staying up too late again, haven't you?"

Now that I'm old, none of these things is my fault. When someone says something about my age spots or the fact that I have put on a little weight or added a bag under each eye, I can lift my eyes heavenward and say, "Oh, dear! (sigh) Things happen to us when we get older. Age, you know. There is nothing I can do."

The body wears out, but the person inside is ageless. I don't look like I did at nineteen, but I am still that dark-haired young woman in spirit. It's a myth that every part of us grows old. The health of most old people is fine, maybe even better than that of young people. Young women catch severe colds, have once-a-month cramps, and suffer from toothaches. Most old people have left those ailments behind.

In addition, don't assume that:

• The elderly don't have much of a social life and feel that they need no friends
• They don't have enough to do
• Loneliness is killing them
• Their health is precarious
• They barely have enough money to get by

The truth is:

They have a lot of friends and they are always eager to meet new people, young and old. They make friends more readily and they have more time now for their friends.

They have plenty to do and most of them are busy doing it. What they're doing may not particularly appeal to a young person, but they are busy.

Loneliness is something most old people have learned to cope with. Mostly because they have no choice. As one woman said, "I'm lonely a good bit of the time, but I console myself with the thought that there are much worse things."

Most old people have more money to spend as they wish than they ever had in their lives. They are not making payments on houses, cars, furniture. They don't feel that they have to buy everything that's on sale. Do you have money left over at the end of the month? They do. Certainly their incomes are reduced and it is a fixed income, but they have learned how to manage.

Because of these myths old people feel a prejudice because of something they can't help and can do nothing about. I have always despised prejudice of any kind and now, for the first time, I am the recipient of it and I know why I have abhorred it so. Sometimes it is very subtle, but that doesn't make it any less painful.

If you can try to understand old people, your caregiving years will be happier. By the time you are old, perhaps the current perception of old age as lonely, unhappy, and nonproductive will be a thing of the past. Won't that be nice for you?

Which brings to mind another myth: that old is old and 'twas ever thus and ever will be. Absolutely not true. This generation of elderly is healthier, smarter, more active mentally and physically than the elderly of only a generation ago. They are living well into their eighties and nineties, and your generation will fare even better.

My friend Flash, in her eighties, went to the hospital for eye surgery. The nurse said, "I'm sorry, but your teeth will have to come out."

"Okay," Flash said, "but you'll have to call my dentist."

The nurse incorrectly assumed that because Flash was old, her teeth were false.

Blow away the myths about old age. Maybe they were true a long time ago, but they aren't true today. Take a second look at your mother and see what she's really like.

CHAPTER 3

Are Your Expectations Unreal?

You love your mother and feel tender and affectionate toward her as she ages. It saddens you to watch her change and diminish in certain ways. The specter of death duels with many other emotions within you.

"Mom's getting old. I love her so much. I'm really concerned about how she's doing."

Words, lady. Not enough. You have an obligation to do more than feel love and express concern. Why isn't love enough? Because it depends on what emotions your love stems from.

If your love and affection are derived from the fact that you are still dependent on your mother, your love is not enough. Why? Because you will be more concerned about yourself and what your mother can do for you than about her needs. Some daughters carry their dependence on their mothers far into adulthood.

If your love and affection are derived from fear, then your love will not be enough. Some grown daughters are scared to death that they will do something to anger or disappoint their mothers. Some mothers know this and use fear as a weapon. Some daughters are afraid of losing their mother's love, perhaps to a sibling who does more for her.

Some are afraid of death. They don't know whether they will be able to cope after their mother dies. These daughters must learn to say, "*When* Mom dies," not "*If* Mom dies." As sure as God made little green apples, mothers die, and the time to face the reality is not at the funeral.

Some daughters' affections are directly proportionate to what their mothers will leave behind. It doesn't necessarily have to be a fortune; they simply want to be sure they get whatever it is.

When you were a little girl, you had certain fears: fear that your mom would leave and never return, fear that she would stop loving you, and fear that she would punish you. Most of us outgrow these fears and develop a different, more equal relationship with our mothers. Some are never able to rid themselves of these childish anxieties. The mother who fosters these fears and uses them to keep her daughter in line will one day be sorry. In her old age she will need a strong, independent caregiver and her daughter won't be able to fill that role.

It is very sad to see adult women trying to live up to their mothers' expectations. No matter how successful they become, how much the world praises them, they feel like failures.

"Mom, I have earned my degree. Now I can practice law."

"That's fine. I wish you would lose some weight."

When I had had several books published, I was asked to speak at various functions. The prospect scared me witless. I was an author, not a speaker! Still, it was a challenge; I discovered I could make a little money; and it helped to sell my books. So I worked very hard at overcoming my stage fright and learning how to speak effectively in public. After several speeches I asked my mother to attend a meeting at which I was the speaker. Not only did I receive a corsage, but there was one for my mother, too. The glowing introduction was wonderful. My speech went off without a hitch, followed by enthusiastic applause. I felt good! On the way home I waited for my mom to say something. When she didn't, I asked, "Well, what did you think?"

"Oh, it was very nice. But I was thinking about your little talk. Why don't you have some kind of a signature sort of thing?"

"A signature thing?"

"Yes. Like, 'That's all, folks!' or well, like Bob Hope's 'Thanks for the memory.' That sort of thing."

The glorious wind blew out of my sails. No one but my mother could deflate me.

"Even fat lawyers make good money, Mom."

It's extremely difficult to brush criticisms of this sort off, but you must. The day will come when your mother will need your caregiving, and if she can make you feel that you are never quite a success, then you won't be able to be what she needs you to be. When she sees that her comments have no power to bother you, she will have to acknowledge the fact that you are grown up.

Sometimes a daughter can't be a good caregiver because she harbors anger toward her mother. If the anger is deep-seated, poor caregiving or no caregiving can be an unconscious form of getting even.

I remember a middle-aged woman telling me about the time her mother gave her bike away. The truth was, she had outgrown the bike, the family was moving and getting rid of unnecessary items, and her parents bought her a new bike soon after the move. Still, to hear this woman tell it, she felt betrayed by her mother's "cruelty" and she nearly lost her trust in people.

We remember spankings ("She beat me for no reason"). We never forget the time mother told us it would be very difficult to become a successful artist (or writer or sculptor). ("I would be a famous artist/author/sculptor today if she hadn't told me I couldn't do it.") We know, in our heart of hearts, that our mother always loved a brother or sister more than she loved us. ("Mary was always her little pet.")

We all exaggerate memories to some extent. The daughters who can't put them in the past where they belong, who can't see the truth now, are the ones who will withhold their caregiving as a means of getting even. ("So, how do *you* like it? Try to get Mary to do it for you.")

Another punishing emotion can get in the way. It's shame. And it comes in many forms. You know you don't do as much for your mother as you could and you're ashamed of yourself. Your brother and/or sister do so much more for Mom than you do and you feel ashamed.

Sometimes we're ashamed of mother because she is too fat, or intellectually inferior, or strongly opinionated, or shabby and poor, or speaks with an accent, or any number of things. And we're ashamed of ourselves for being ashamed. So our caregiving is inadequate because we tend to turn our backs on situations that make us feel ashamed. But ignoring a need won't make it go away. These negative feelings have to be faced, evaluated, and dealt with.

Shame about yourself and your mother will make you feel guilty. That's piling another negative feeling on top of the others. I have heard it so often: "I tried to do as much as I could for Mom, but it was never enough. I felt so guilty!" Could it be that it was never enough as far as *you* were concerned? Are you sure it wasn't enough for your mother?

Look for a talent or quality that offsets the thing that makes you ashamed, and build on it.

"My mom doesn't read much and isn't up on current affairs, but have you ever tasted her cherry pie?"

Take a good look at your guilt. It may very well be that you have nothing to feel guilty about. Or your mother may be purposely trying to make you feel guilty. In that case, make up your mind that she won't get away with it. One woman wrote, "My mother died recently and freed me from eighteen years of guilt." Don't wait for her death to release you.

When my children were little and did something they shouldn't have done, they would look up at me with tear-filled eyes (after being caught in the act). "I'm sorry!" they wailed. I always responded by saying, "Show me." They had to prove to me that they were sorry with their actions, not their words. That's what they would face in the real world, and it was my job to prepare them.

"Until the day Mom died, I called her every single day." That fact makes you feel good. But what if your mother knew that every phone call was a duty call? That you were always doing something else: cooking, watching TV, and so on, with the phone snuggled under your chin? You seldom listened, always patronized her. Your visits to her home were few and far between. Yes, you called her every day and you told her that you loved her. Was it enough?

What about your expectations? Can you ever do enough for your mother? Can you be sure that, after she dies, you will have no regrets? If you love your mother and do the best you can for her, it will be enough. The mother-daughter relationship involves a lot of tension, but no one will ever love you and accept you in exactly the same way your mother does. You know this, and when the caregiving years go on and it gets rough at times, remind yourself of this beautiful truth. No matter how it goes, what mistakes you make, your mother will die loving you and insisting that you were the best caregiving daughter who ever walked the face of this earth.

CHAPTER 4

Grow Up and Let Go

Old people lose so much as the years go by. Besides the physical losses and degeneration, they lose mate, friends, social status.

Not long ago, when her brother died, my ninety-four-year-old mother-in-law said, "Now I'm the last apple on the tree." I could feel her sadness. She had seen all of her family die, and she was next. If you live long enough, you will be the last apple on the tree.

However, something wonderful, almost miraculous, happens. Old people start to let go. They don't let go of life, or hope. They don't give up and resign themselves to a bleak old age. Far from it. However, they do start to let go of their love for and attachment to things. They must, or the prospect of their death would be absolutely unbearable. If you continued to care so very much for people and things, you would be in turmoil and you would be unable to accept your impending death. I have seen old people on their deathbeds, screaming and raging at what was happening to them. It was pitiful. They had failed at the art of letting go.

If your mother refuses to let go, you can help. First of all, don't indulge her when she makes statements like "I'm not old. I'm only as old as I feel." Tell her, "Of course you're old, but you're such a beautiful old lady. I hope I can be old in exactly the same way you are."

A friend of mine insisted she was not old. She kept her hair dyed a dark brown, she dieted constantly, and she held doors for me and insisted on carrying my packages. She was exactly two years younger than me, so she certainly was not a young person! I humored her, but I felt sorry for her daughter because she told me that she felt as though she were in competition with her mother.

There is absolutely nothing wrong with a woman having a face-lift or a tuck here and there. If gray hair distresses a woman, she can buy marvelous tints and dyes to cover it up. However, the masquerading has to stop sometime because the ravages of old age won't be denied forever.

The old woman who accepts her advancing years and concentrates on being gracious and charming and loving has plenty going for her.

As your mother's caregiver, remember to compliment her now and then. Rave about how beautiful silver hair is. (It is!) Admit that she has earned every line and wrinkle in her face. Stand in awe of anyone who has lived more than (or nearly) three-quarters of a century. You won't have to pretend. If you think about these things, you will realize they're true.

Old people begin by letting go of little things. One mother who had always treasured her small collection of jewelry called her three daughters in one day and told them to divide the pieces among themselves. "But, Mom," they protested, "your jewelry! Why are you doing this?" Their mother shrugged and replied, "That stuff is just not very important to me anymore. I would rather you girls enjoy it."

Some months before my mother's sudden death she threw away cards, letters, and pictures. It frightened me because it seemed that she had a premonition of her death. "Oh, no," she said, "nothing like that. I just don't care about keeping these things anymore." She was letting go.

You have to be mature to begin to understand and sympathize with this letting-go process. Following is a quiz to rate your maturity:

1. *If you try very hard to be nice and if you are unselfish and loving, then everyone will love you.*

If you think that, you're a baby. The mature adult knows where she is going and pretty much how she is going to get there. She is a nice person, certainly, and has principles and morals, but she does not delude herself. You may be doing the best caregiving in the world, but siblings will criticize and be jealous, and even your mother will be annoyed with you at times. Take it in stride. "I'm doing the best I can. If you know a better way, tell me about it. I'll listen. Whether you like me or approve of what I'm doing isn't all that important."

2. *Mom is Mom, the same old Mom she has always been. She is there for me in so many ways. After all, that's what moms are for.*

Oh, no, it isn't! Stop and take another look. You are grown up now and should be able to see your mother as someone besides your mommy. Your mother is a person with dreams and hopes and visions of her own. Some of her dreams have shattered or faded, some have died on the vine, but all have affected her. She may be old, but she still has dreams. Treat her as a person.

3. *If I try hard and don't mess up, everything will turn out okay.*

Grown-up babies sit around and cry, "But that's not fair!" while mature adults never expected it to be fair in the first place. They cope. Maybe you're experiencing menopause, your kids are giving you trouble, and your husband has that itch he gets about every seven years. And you have your mother to care for. So you must cope. Pray and do the best you can. Be as good to yourself as possible. Don't even think about whether it's fair. When has life ever been fair?

4. *If I study and think and observe and work at this caregiving role, I will have all the answers.*

Have you ever talked to a young person who had all the answers? The conversation is dotted with "Yes, but . . ." and "Of course. Only . . ." It's tiresome. And it's juvenile. The mature adult is able to say, "Tell me what you think," and to learn from others. You may know a lot, but you don't know everything. Instead of doing what you think is best for your mother all the time, now and then ask her what she wants. You are probably in for a surprise.

5. *No matter what Mom asks me to do, I simply can't say no to her. After all, she's my mother.*

Are you afraid of her? You should have outgrown that attitude a long time ago. Listen to your mother, give her your full attention and respect, but if she is too demanding, say to her, "I'm sorry, Mom, but it's very inconvenient for me to do that." Then let it go. Your mother will accept your refusal because she has to. After all, she's a mature adult too.

6. *A lot of my problems are because we were so poor (or so rich) when I was growing up. My mother never gave me*

enough freedom (or too much), didn't pay enough attention to me (or smothered me). I know she loved me, but if she had done it differently, I would be a better and happier person today.

Baloney! What a cop-out mentality. It's time to forgive and forget. Think about it. Do you want your children to harbor all the mistakes they think you're making and throw them all back in your face when you're old? Your mother did love you and she did the best she could with what she had. Instead of thinking about all you missed, like a petulant child, be grateful for all you had. On the other hand, if your mother really did mistreat and abuse you, go to a psychiatrist.

I hope that these questions have helped you gauge your maturity and will prompt you to proceed in your caregiving in an adult way.

CHAPTER 5

The Supercaregiver

Right from the beginning, drop the notion that you're going to have to be Superwoman. It's not a goal you should aim for. It's too exhausting and not at all necessary. Because you're really not a superwoman, eventually you'll resent the responsibilities, and later on it may be nearly impossible to return to normal. Husband, children, and your mother will very quickly get used to this superwoman and begin to take you for granted.

Why do we pile it on, load after load, until we're crying, "Enough already!"?

Guilt. We certainly don't overextend ourselves because we love rushing our heads off, waiting on everyone, being a slave. Nor do we do it because we think we'll receive some great reward, either here or in heaven.

Help your mother when and if she needs help and don't help her too much. Be there when she does need you, but back off most of the time. You can't do this with young children, but you must with your mother.

Giving up her independence, regardless of the reason, would be the final, tragic surrender for your mother. Someday she may have to, but don't you hasten the day by trying to be supercaregiver.

CHAPTER 6

Excess Baggage

Some years ago I was asked to give a program in a church. The theme was "Pulling Together," and how the church would prosper if its members worked together.

I came on stage absolutely loaded down with plastic trash bags. I pretended they were heavy by huffing and puffing and dragging them along. (Actually they were stuffed with paper.)

"Don't ask me to work for the church," I said. "I have all this to carry around. Take this bag—it represents the time I was so sick and the pastor never called on me. He said later he hadn't known I was sick, but I didn't think that was much of an excuse. My feelings were so hurt! This is a heavy bag to carry around, but I can't get rid of it."

"This other bag represents the time I worked so hard on plans for the church bake sale and the ladies decided on another plan at the last minute, without even telling me. I can't forgive them for that, so I have to carry this bag around too." And on and on.

We all burden ourselves with emotional baggage. Someone cheated us or didn't invite us to their party. We carry these little slights and insults around for years. They're excess baggage, but we are hesitant to unload it.

Excess baggage stemming from the mother-daughter relationship is heavier than others. The emotion between mother and daughter is unique. It can be beautiful, comforting, shared, tender, mutually supporting. It can also be competitive, demanding, cruel, hurtful, stormy, and sad. At different times in our lives we have experienced all of these emotions.

Regardless of how it is with you and your mother, as she grows older, it probably won't get better and it may get worse. Your mother may go on for a very long time needing only minimal caregiving, but a heart attack, a stroke, or a bad fall could transform the relationship overnight.

This is one reason why you shouldn't make promises. Promises are emotional baggage and can become burdensome. Don't say, "Mom, you and I will always have every Wednesday together to shop or go to a movie." Maybe you won't always be available on Wednesdays. If your mother asks you to promise that you will do something, tell her you hope you will be able to do what she wishes. Make commitments, not promises. When you commit yourself to your mother's welfare, you are saying that you will do whatever you have to do, whatever is possible, in whatever situation that arises. You and she know that you will honor your commitment.

You may think that sometimes your mother acts like a child. Maybe she does, but if you can't understand it and you allow it to bother you, that's more baggage you have to tote. Don't treat her like a child, because nine times out of ten she has a good reason for her actions. Surely you can forgive the tenth time.

Heide takes me grocery shopping once a week. We go to the library, out for lunch, to the fabric and book stores. When we started this habit, I noticed that she was driving too fast and tailgating, and it made me nervous. On several occasions I asked her to slow down.

She didn't, so one day when she stopped at a red light, I got out of the car. I told her I would call a taxi.

That made her angry. "I don't see how you can be so childish, Mama."

It wasn't childish at all. I had to get my point across.

Now it only takes a gentle reminder to get her to ease up on the gas. (How she drives when I'm not in the car is her business.) I brought my concern out into the open, we dealt with it, and we eliminated that excess baggage.

Caregiving used to be thought of only in terms of caring for children. For most of us, raising children is a good, happy responsibility. We get results. The children grow and learn and become less and less in need of our caregiving, until they are able to make a life for themselves. This process is very satisfying.

Caregiving of the elderly is not the same; and you should be aware of this fact. The elderly grow more dependent, and their road leads to death. You are investing money and time and care in someone who doesn't have much of a future. Accept that reality.

Nevertheless you still feel sad and frustrated watching your dear parent grow weaker and less independent. Your mother is a constant reminder of what is going to happen to you eventually, and you can't be blamed for preferring not to see it staring you in the face day after day.

Well, that's too bad! Why not look at your caregiving as the last sharing, caring, loving thing you and your mother will experience together and savor every moment of it? If you look at it in that light, you will want it to be gentle and loving and meaningful. Surround your mother with love; vow to enrich the experience. And pray that one day, because of your example, your kids will do the same for you.

The mother-daughter relationship is intense. Still, or maybe because of its strength, you once felt an overpowering need to break away from your mother. "I have my own life to live!" you cried, meaning that you needed to break away from that powerful interdependence in order to become your own person.

When you were a little girl, your mother's approval was your sunshine, while her disapproval made your stomach churn. You never quite lose that need for your mother's approval. You didn't marry the man your mother hoped you would; your housekeeping is far below her standards; you don't dress the way she thinks young ladies should dress. You can't live your own life if you are in desperate need of your mother's approval. You may need to reenact that scene from your teenage years somehow and let your mother know that you are going to live your life the way you want to live it.

Mother and daughter will never completely agree on everything. You are adult individuals with different ideas and views about many things. The fact is, your mother's authority is always present, no matter how old you are. It sits between you and colors the words and actions of both of you.

I remember watching my grown daughter eat and getting quite upset about the way she was going about it. She ate all the vegetables on her plate. Then she ate a roll. Then she drank her tea. Finally she ate the meat.

"That is not the proper way to eat," I said.

"What's wrong with it?"

"You're supposed to eat it all together, not one thing at a time."

"This is the way I like to do it."

"But it's not correct. You were certainly taught differently."

She shrugged, smiled, and went on eating the meat.

"I only hope that when you're eating in a nice place, with people who know their manners, you won't forget how you were raised."

Then my daughter said, "Well, Mama, this is me. It's how I am. You don't have to worry about it."

I was never so proud of her. She was telling me that she was grown up, that we both had opinions and that that was okay. She was also telling me, in a nice way, to mind my own business. To me, that meant that we could be friends.

In order to have a good, healthy relationship with your mother, you have to handle this power she exerted over you in your youth intelligently. To some extent, she will have it as long as she lives. Also, as long as you allow it, your mother will use it. If you don't allow it, you and your mother can take the next step toward a more mature relationship. Your mother may be surprised at first, but she will be happier in the long run. Both you and your mother have to adapt and try to understand these shifting roles.

When there is understanding and cooperation, your mother will go on loving and appreciating you even though you are independent and have cut the apron strings. You will love your mother as always and maintain great respect for her, but you will simply refuse to let her run your life. When you have both rid yourselves of this emotional baggage, you can enjoy the caregiving years as mature women who love each other.

If you're carrying the baggage of a fear of letting your mother know where you stand, the solution may be simply speaking up to her, regardless of her disapproval.

When Heide was dating and living at home, she chose not to tell me about certain things that happened in her life. It was her decision and her right. She was an adult, and if she felt that some things were none of my business, then they were none of my business. I was aware of this and accepted it.

Oddly enough, once she was married and had taken on the role of my caregiver, I wanted to know everything going on in her life. I wanted to be absolutely sure that "my baby" was happy. My mothering instinct was born again and I asked Heide if she was eating properly, getting enough sleep, having any fun. I love my son-in-law, so it had nothing to do with any criticism of him. I simply turned into Mother Hen clucking over her chick.

One day I went too far. Heide had been putting up with my unfamiliar attitude long enough. We were walking down the aisle of a department store. I said, "You're doing too much. Besides doing the cooking and cleaning and laundry you're working at a full-time job."

"It's okay. I'm fine."

"You're going to wear yourself out before you're thirty."

"I said I'm okay. I'm doing fine."

"It's just that I would like for life to be a little easier for you."

With a great deal of patience Heide steered me down another aisle and tried to change the subject.

Except that the aisle she steered me down contained microwave ovens. I stopped in front of one. "A microwave oven would make your life a lot easier, Heide."

"True. But we can't afford one right now."

Like an avalanche I kept rolling. "I'll be glad to buy one for you."

Heide stopped walking, turned and faced me, and looked into my eyes. "I don't want you to buy me a microwave oven."

"You can call it an early birthday gift."

"Mama, I don't know what's come over you. I am not your little girl. I'm a married woman and, believe it or not,

I'm doing just fine. You don't have to fuss and worry about me. I know you love me, but you make me feel that you have no confidence in me."

Her response was like a slap in the face, but it was a slap I needed. I hadn't realized I was undermining her, acting as though she couldn't take care of herself.

That's all there was to it. Heide said no more and neither did I. We moved away from the microwave ovens, and the rest of the day was pleasant.

I know that Heide hated talking to me as she did, but she knew it was something she had to do. She couldn't be an adequate caregiver with me fussing and fretting over her as though she were a child. We never mentioned the subject again, but I did a lot of thinking and I revised my attitude toward my adult, married daughter. On the day she said to me, "Hey, we bought a microwave oven today," we exchanged smiles that said volumes.

I know too many mothers who continue to treat their adult daughters as though they were still little girls. Some of these daughters allow this behavior either out of greed (look at all the goodies mommies buy for good little girls) or because they are afraid to speak up. By allowing their mothers to treat them like youngsters, they are giving their mothers a power they have no right to. Somewhere down the line, when these mothers need their daughters to be caregivers, the daughters are going to be so out of control they won't be able to function as caregivers. They will be the little girls crying, "Mommy, I need you!" when the truth is their mothers will need them.

I know an elderly woman who hated a certain hairstyle. Naturally her daughter loved it, but when she was with her mother, she braided her hair and twisted it into a knot. "I know you hate that hairstyle, Mom, so I braided my hair."

Her daughter's actions made that mother feel guilty, and it showed that her daughter needed her mother's approval far too much. Her mother would have been much more comfortable if her daughter had worn the modern style and said, "I know you hate this hairstyle, Mom, but I like it. Didn't you ever do anything that your mother didn't approve of?"

If you want to be friends with your mother (and isn't it about time?), mind your manners. Be as polite to her as you are to your friends. (Would a friend put up with a temper tantrum when things don't go your way?)

If your mother fails to mind her manners by exercising her maternal authority, tell her. Do it in a loving way, but let her know that she's out of line.

If a friend tries bossing you around, or criticizing everything you do, you tell her off. "Hey, cut that out. I don't appreciate that." You talk, maybe argue, clear the air, and the friendship isn't damaged.

My friend Flash and I will be talking up a storm and she keeps interjecting her thoughts. I say, "Stop interrupting me!"

"I'm not. You talk so much I have to try to get a word in edgewise." So I stop talking so much, she stops interrupting, and on we go.

Do the same with your mother. When she makes you angry, don't stomp off like you did when you were a little girl. (Or whatever it was you did when you were a little girl.) Tell her what she said or did and why it upset you. Be calm and loving, but get your message across: You're a big girl and you're not afraid of her. You might have to change a few things before you can pull this off. I saw a forty-year-old woman say to her mother, "Stop treating me like a child!" Her sixty-two-year-old mother glared at her. "How can you talk to me like that after all I do for you?" The daughter lowered her eyes and said nothing more. It was a very sad scene. If only she would have said, "Mom, you don't have to do so much for me. Let me do nice things for you."

If a friend is more knowledgeable than you on a subject, you ask her advice, just as she asks you for direction on things you know more about. That's a part of the give-and-take of friendship. Do this with your mother. Ask her advice, providing you're willing to take it. You don't have to take it, understand, just be willing to.

"Mom, I got this thing in the mail. Do you think it's for real, or is it a scam?" Your mother has lived a long time, she has seen scams come and go, and she's a pretty smart cookie. Listen to what she says. Nine times out of ten, you'll be glad you did.

One old lady was frustrated and unhappy because her daughter asked for her advice on many things but seldom took it.

"Should I buy this, Mom?"

Her mother carefully considered it, looked at all the possibilities, and gave the best answer she knew. "No, I don't think that would be a wise purchase." She stated her reasons. Remember, her opinion was requested.

A few weeks later that woman was in her daughter's home and there sat the item. The next time she is asked, she will probably refuse to give any advice. It would have been much better for the daughter to say, "I understand what you're saying, and you're probably right, but I think I'll buy it anyway," than to pretend to take her mother's advice and then go ahead and do what she pleased. You don't have to do anything behind your mother's back. Secrecy is not indicative of an adult relationship.

Even though you are your mother's daughter and you are her caregiver, you can be friends. When my daughters were little girls, then teenagers, I had no desire to be their friend. "I'm your mother," I reminded them. Back then it was important to exercise my authority.

Now it's different and we can be friends. You have to stop treating your mother like your mommy. You may have to make your mother stop acting like a mommy.

First of all, don't seek her approval of everything you do. Approve of yourself. Give yourself permission to do what you think is best, what pleases you. Allow yourself to make mistakes. You cannot live your life for anyone but yourself. By the time your mother reaches old age—and death—you should be standing firmly on your own two feet. You can rest assured that that is the way your mother wants it.

I had a friend who never told me much about herself. Figuring she didn't like talking about herself, I didn't reveal very much about myself. Our friendship continued for several years, but we were never close. Then a tragedy hit her family. The floodgates opened and I was there. I cried with her and held her in my arms. Later I told her of some of the heartbreaks in my life. Since that day we have been very close, and we confide in each other, accept each other, and love each other more every day.

If you and your mother can't open up to each other, if you don't know your mother as a person with dreams and hopes and memories, something precious is missing in your relationship.

When I told my kids about going to a radio station in Chicago when I was young and lying about my age in order to get in and meet my idol, Dave Garroway, they were impressed. "You did that, Mom?" They saw me in a different light. I suppose they had never before thought of me as a silly, hero-worshipping teenager. Share thoughts and experiences and memories with each other and become friends.

There are other kinds of mothers: The Saint Joan type—

they love to play the martyr ("I was sick all week, but I know how busy you are with that husband of yours, so I didn't bother you."). Or the Little Four-Star General ("I told you not to do that. How could you be so stupid? You never listen to me."). Or the Witch-on-a-Broomstick ("Why can't you keep your house neater, and your children should not wear jeans all the time. Didn't I raise you to be neat, for goodness sake?").

I will tell you what you can do about all of these. What you can't do is change your mother. Accept that fact. Then work on yourself. You will have to react to her in a way that is easy on you. You can't control your mother, but you can control your feelings and reactions so that you don't become her victim.

Understand that Saint Joan is making a bid for attention. Do what you can do. Be sympathetic and loving, but stay in control. "I am so sorry you had a headache, Mom. Take some aspirin and lie down. I'll see you as usual on Thursday."

The Little Four-Star General and the Witch-on-a-Broomstick don't have to get you tied up in knots either. Live your life as it pleases you and your family, and learn to let your mother's criticisms go in one ear and out the other. She is not going to stop making her critical remarks and you are not going to change into what she thinks you should be, so don't be afraid to be assertive. Tell her to stop. Or simply walk away.

It's time that you were in control of yourself. Sometimes a person—particularly a woman—is in control in every area of life except her dealings with her mother. Take charge of your life, but also remember to let your mother know that you love her, even though you won't allow her to run your life. Say "I love you" often. You know in your heart that you love her and you assume that she knows it, too. It's a shame when the words aren't said enough. "I love you" is one of the sweetest expressions in the English language. ("A word aptly spoken is like apples of gold in settings of silver."—Proverbs 25:11)

Your children came into this world as raw material, as did we all. You had to care for them, teach them, feed them, help them grow until they were ready to live on their own.

Your mother did not enter old age unprepared. She was already an accumulation of years of growing, learning, and experiencing. The whole of her past life, the events she lived through, and her responses to those events make up what she is now.

Your job is not to train or teach or help her grow. As her caregiver you only need to help make her remaining years as pleasant and safe and easy and love-filled as you can. You won't be able to do it unless you're a mature adult who can accept your mother as a person. In fact if you're still looking and reacting to her as the little girl to her mommy, you can't be her caregiver at all. You are both straining under too heavy a load that is nothing more than emotional baggage.

CHAPTER 7

When You and Your
Mother Don't Get Along

A lot of caregiving is done mostly out of a sense of guilt. Not guilt, but a *sense* of guilt, and the two are entirely different. When you feel guilty, it's because you have done something wrong. A sense of guilt is a vague unrest within. "Am I bad because I didn't do that? Should I have done more?" Some caregivers believe that they must do for their parents everything their parents did for them. Caregiving becomes payment of a debt they think they owe.

If your caregiving is to be meaningful, you have to get rid of the guilt and feelings of debt. Your caregiving should be borne out of love and your enjoyment in being with your mother.

However, what if you and your mother never got along? Perhaps she never got along with anyone in the family. Or it may be that advancing age has turned your mother into a nagger, a complainer, a demanding tyrant. Maybe she argues bitterly with you and your siblings. She complains about everything you do. Nothing pleases her, nothing will satisfy. Over the years you have become more or less reconciled to her orneriness, largely by staying away from her. Now that she's old, she needs some caregiving and you can't abandon her. How do you handle this? You could stand it for a few weeks, or even months, but we're talking years.

I have received many letters from both elderly mothers and caregiving daughters that speak of this sad situation:

"I am the one who needs my daughter's love. I suppose it's my fault, but she obviously doesn't want my love."

"My daughter and I have never been close. She would never even call me if guilt didn't overtake her on occasion."

"I have taken care of my mother for eight years and all I can say is that she is one big pain in the neck."

"My mother played every manipulative game on me that you can think of."

"My mother put me through twenty-seven years of guilt making."

Now, it just happens that you are the only one in the family who lives near your mother, so you are automatically elected her caregiver. Very often one person—almost always a daughter—become's Mom's principal caregiver without any discussion or planning. She may be the only one living near the mother, or brothers and sisters may refuse to accept the role. Even when all siblings live nearby, usually only one person acquires the role of primary caregiver.

The best solution would be to hire someone and to settle for an occasional phone call or visit. You could keep a careful check on this caregiver to be sure your mother was properly cared for, but you wouldn't have to put yourself through the unpleasant arguing and complaining. The only trouble with this wonderful solution is that very few can afford it. If you do decide to go this route, be careful about whom you hire. Check references. Just because a person has been trained to care for the elderly doesn't guarantee that person's honesty or integrity. He may steal from your mother or may be cruel in little ways. (See Resources for home care.)

One caregiver wrote, "I go to my mom's with the best intentions. In no time we're screaming at each other and I leave, and I'm so angry and I take it out on my husband and kids."

Another: "I try to help my mother. Every time I do, hoping she'll be pleased, she accuses me of butting in. She tells me I'm interfering and she makes me feel terrible. I always leave with tears in my eyes."

You have to try to understand why your mother is as she is. Search your memory, talk to your brothers and sisters and other relatives. Try to dig up the truth, because it might make it possible for you to understand, maybe even to sympathize. One fact is certain: You are never going to change your mother, so don't even venture down that path.

One woman never wanted children. Her husband had other ideas, so she had five. To her dying day she resented them. This woman was cold and mean to her children, but they didn't have to take on a load of guilt. Her temper wasn't their fault.

Look at yourself. Are you sure that at least part of the problem isn't something you do—or don't do? One caregiving daughter, trying to be helpful, checked her mother's pantry, refrigerator, freezer, and bathroom cabinets every time she went to her mother's house. Her actions angered her mother, who told her daughter so. But the daughter said, "I'm only checking to see what you need" and kept on doing it. That one thing unraveled and nearly destroyed their relationship.

You and your mother can go to a clergyperson, a doctor, or a friend you both trust for counseling and therapy. Sometimes a person on the outside can evaluate the problem objectively and suggest a solution.

If nothing works, and healing appears improbable, about the best you can do is to talk to your mother, state the rules (your rules), and call a truce. Tell her you will give her minimal care. You will do what you have to do to protect her health and life and nothing else.

Or you can tell her that she will have to pay for her care—as much as she can afford—and that you will foot the bills she can't pay for.

Or you can get together with your siblings and insist that they share in the caregiving. No matter where they live, your mother either stays with them for part of the year or they have to pay a professional for an agreed-upon period of time. No excuses. Make it perfectly clear to all, including your mother, that you will not put up with a demanding, complaining, critical mother and let them off free.

You can't desert her. No matter how intolerable she is, she is your mother. You have to be able to live with yourself. So you have to be smart. Make sure that your mother is cared for, but that you are not doing *everything*, and remember that you and your family come first, except in a life-or-death situation.

What a sad thing discord is! But let's not fool ourselves that it doesn't exist. Animosity occurs more often than we care to think, with many variations and to differing degrees. Please don't try to firm up your little chin, wipe the tears away, and strive to do your very best for your mother whether or not it kills you. Living under stress for years does kill.

Many modern caregivers become dependent on drugs or alcohol, or suffer from depression, colitis, headaches, backaches, and ulcers. All because they worry about aging parents and because they don't feel secure in their role of caregiver. When you add constant arguing and complaining and sulkiness to the strain, the caregiver is in real danger.

The Bible says that a soft answer turns away wrath (Proverbs 15:1). It's true. I used to get quite upset when clerks and waiters were impolite to me, when they didn't smile or talk pleasantly. So I would let them have a taste of my anger. I seldom got more than a sarcastic apology and I always walked away angry. In later years I have discovered that a smile and soft words melt nearly everyone. The clerk snaps at me and I smile and say, "I guess you've had a bad day. This must be a tough job." Every single time, I am rewarded with a smile and a courteous answer. Maybe you could try this with your mother. Turn away her curt remarks with a soft response. It can't hurt and it might help. At least it will be easier on you.

We have all seen or heard about the woman who stands beside her mother's casket. Her tears are bitter and copious. "If only I had been nicer to my mother, if only I'd tried harder, and now it's too late." That woman will never, as long as she lives, entirely get over the sorrow in her heart.

You don't want that to happen to you. It won't because of any lack of love or caring on your part. It won't because you didn't try. But unless you work at personality clashes, unless you diligently try to overcome frictional episodes, you may later feel that you bungled the job of caregiving. Even though you may have all the right on your side, and your mother is wrong, make her last years as pleasant as possible—for your own sake.

SECTION II

Getting Down
to Business

*"Even to your old age I am He,
and to gray hairs I will carry you.
I have made, I will bear."*

ISAIAH 46:4

CHAPTER 8

Finances

Most of us are content with enough money to pay our bills and keep a roof overhead and food in the pantry. Now, for many, enough also to care for an aging mother is needed.

The Bible says it's the love of money that is the root of evil (1 Timothy 6:10), not money itself. Where there is love of money for money's sake, there is greed and jealousy and even murder. All most of us want is enough to pay our way without worrying about how we're going to do it.

Back in those olden days when parents didn't live for many years beyond retirement, money wasn't much of a problem. Most parents were frugal and dedicated to saving money so that "we have something to leave the children."

Oh, boy, how times have changed. Mothers are living well into their eighties and nineties and the children are in their fifties and sixties and probably well established financially. At least they are able to take care of themselves and their families. Some caregivers and their spouses are finding themselves spending money on Mom that they saved for their own retirement.

Do you know what your mother's financial situation is? Old people are often secretive and sometimes ashamed about this, usually because they don't want you to know how little they are getting by on. Some don't want you to know how much they have because they don't want to spend any of it. You can find out and figure out what her expenses are and about how much she has left over. She may be doing very well, or she may be hurting. If she's hurting, do not hand her money. An old lady's worst fear is being a burden to her children. You will have to work it out in some clever (all right, sneaky) way. One lady wrote, "I am seventy-two years old and I live on a farm. I'm rather isolated, especially during our long, snowy winters. What I really want to do is sell the farm and move to Arizona, but I'm afraid to do that because I might spend too much money or make some terrible mistake and become a burden to my children." I picture that woman enduring those long, lonely winters year after year simply because she's afraid to take a chance and maybe become a financial burden to her children. She and her children should come up with a solution that is sensible and pleasing to the mother.

Another woman said, "I tell my kids that I never worry about finances because I'm worth a fortune. I have silver in my hair, gold in my teeth, stones in my kidneys, lead in my feet, and gas in my stomach."

Whether your mother has a lot of money or a little, problems can arise.

You have to get down to brass tacks concerning your mother's financial status. How will medical bills be paid? Figure out exactly what her assets are. Does she want to give you power of attorney now so that you can handle her affairs if she can't? Ask a lawyer about durable power of attorney and explain it to your mother. Or both of you talk to a lawyer before your mother makes any decision.

For example, perhaps your mother has given you power

of attorney and has written a Living Will. However, the power of attorney will become invalid if your mother becomes incompetent. A durable power of attorney is more flexible. Your mother can state her exact and precise wishes concerning treatment if she becomes ill and if she becomes incompetent, you will still retain durable power of attorney.

Some people will openly discuss religion, politics, and their sex life but never the amount of their paycheck. Your mother may be secretive about how much money she has because she feels (perhaps rightly so) that her children only want to know how much they can expect to get when she dies. If this is true, it hurts your mother a lot, and the least she can do is keep the kids guessing.

Some old people say, "I'm leaving nothing to my children. I'm going to live long enough to spend it all." That used to be a joke; today it's more of a reality.

However, some still feel that an inheritance for their children is important. They will go without in order to have money to leave their children. If you don't already know, find out your mother's plans about her savings. Don't try to change her, work with her.

You must bring your mother's financial picture out in the open and talk about it. At the first stage it should be between only you—the caregiver—and your mother. It's no one else's business. Later, when you and your mother have studied it and made some decisions, then you should let other family members know what those plans are. Perhaps they only need to be given a general picture, but they should be informed. How much they should be told will depend on your relationship with your siblings, if they will be expected to contribute, and if it's all right with your mother.

Don't adopt the attitude that your mother is incapable of handling her finances. Rather, explain that you both have to look ahead and plan. She may be due benefits that she isn't aware of. Let her make the decisions, but as her caregiver you have a right to determine how her caregiving will be paid for both now and in the future. You have the right because the burden, if she becomes ill, will fall on you, and lack of planning could be disastrous.

It would be a good idea to become an alternate signator to your mother's checking and savings accounts so that you have emergency withdrawal and check-writing authority. Keep spare checks and withdrawal slips from both accounts on hand.

Your mother has probably worked outside the home, has balanced her own checkbook, established credit, made major purchases. You are not needed to boss her around or take over her finances. All you need to do is lay out the possibility of future crises and determine how they will be paid for. Then, if necessary, plan with your mother ways to make sure that money will be available and establish the source of that money.

Be careful. You want to ascertain your mother's financial status and whether or not you can help make it more secure, but your mother may have different ideas. One woman's daughter thought her widowed mother should move from her spacious, three-bedroom apartment to a one-bedroom and save at least three hundred dollars a month. It made sense because after the last child married, that extra space wasn't needed. Her mother had entirely different ideas. One of the bedrooms was the mother's study, where she painted and wrote poetry. The other extra bedroom was a guest room, and she had plans for inviting old friends to visit her. Besides, she enjoyed having space for her furniture and to move around in. It was worth the extra three hundred dollars a month for her to have these things. Whether it made sense to her daughter or not, it was her mother's choice and her mother's money.

Another woman, much to her caregiving daughter's distress, refused to spend money on herself. There was plenty of money for her mother to live very comfortably, but the caregiver had to stand helplessly by while her mother mended and remended slips and dresses and ate only the cheapest foods. This mother wanted to be sure she left money to her children, and her daughter could not do much about it.

Another woman, quite wealthy, told her daughter that she had taken care of everything. Her funeral was prepaid, she had plenty of health insurance, and all of her bills were paid. "So it's none of your business what I have or don't have," she said. After she died, it was discovered that she had left all of her money to charity. A note explained that since her son-in-law had been so hateful to her, she was making sure that he did not benefit from her death in any way.

Realize first that it is your mother's money and she can do exactly as she pleases. Your only goal is to help her if she needs help, make sure she is getting all she's entitled to, and determine how a sickness, hospitalization, nursing-home care, and her funeral will be paid for. If you discover that you will have to pay for at least part of it, you can start planning now.

You may have some particular concerns that should be aired:

• You may feel cheated because you are the one shouldering the entire burden.
• You may feel cheated because you do all the work and running around for your mother, while your siblings think

a check now and then discharges their responsibility. Or one sibling visits and calls your mother on a regular basis, while another sends checks—do their gestures balance out?

• Your siblings may be annoyed because they think you call all the shots since you contribute the most.

• You do all the work, have all the responsibility. You and your siblings share equally in Mom's will. (It doesn't matter that the inheritance may consist of a few dollars, some dishes, silver, and furniture. These possessions acquire a symbolic value far beyond their actual worth.)

• Your mother is healthy and, according to statistics, will live for many more years. As long as she remains healthy, Social Security and her small pension are enough. But if she becomes ill, or falls and breaks a bone, or becomes too frail to live alone, will the money be enough?

If these concerns bother you, seek answers and discover your options.

If your mother knows little about monetary matters, probably because her husband took care of everything financial, you can (a) teach her how to do these things; or (b) take it all out of her hands. Let this be your mother's decision.

Find out if your mother has health insurance and/or Medicare. Very carefully examine all the benefits so that you will know how fully she's covered.

A note of warning: There are insurance scams targeted to older people. Advise your mother to be cautious. Some of the worst abuses are in the form of door-to-door salesmen peddling so-called Medi-Gap and cancer insurance to the elderly. Lonely old people are particularly susceptible to this kind of scam because they welcome someone who talks to them and seems to care about them.

How much will your mother's savings account actually be worth five, ten, fifteen years from now? Stay abreast of inflation and changes. What is true today may be obsolete tomorrow. Is the money in your mother's savings account earning as much money as possible? Talk to your banker.

It's true that the minute your dad dies your mom's financial status takes a nosedive. The intent of Social Security back in 1935 was to provide security after retirement. That's not true today. Inflation has changed that picture. If you have questions, visit or call your local Social Security office with your mother. It will have the answers.

Look into SSI—Supplemental Security Income. It is not charity. This is a supplement to Social Security that provides money for disabled, aged, and blind people who do not have adequate resources. Qualifications must be met. Eligibility for SSI is determined by the amount of income, savings, and property. Actual amounts change.

One woman receiving three hundred dollars a month from Social Security may do quite well. She also receives money from her late husband's pension fund and has rental property that provides additional income. Another woman receiving three hundred dollars from Social Security will be below the poverty level if there is no other income. If you think your mother may be eligible for SSI, call your local Social Security office and find out. Better yet, suggest to your mother that she call.

How well your mother fares on her income depends also on where she lives. A woman living in a small town in Texas, for instance, will be content on five hundred dollars a month. A woman living in the Los Angeles area would have barely enough to rent a one-room apartment.

You may or may not be legally responsible for your

mother's bills and upkeep (your Social Security office can tell you), but you may feel a moral obligation. If you do, it's yours, legal or not. So how can you help your mother and, in the long run, help yourself?

1. See a lawyer or financial adviser. It might be a good idea, for example, to have your mother's house put in your name so that it can't be possessed to pay bills. The laws vary in different states and you must have professional advice. You and your mother need to stay informed in regard to the many changes that occur. She may be entitled to additional income, but she won't get it unless she applies for it.

There are other sources of income. The federally funded Senior Companion program, for example, pays low-income elderly $2.20 an hour to assist the homebound frail elderly. A healthy sixty-eight-year-old can visit someone who is ninety or older. Check with your local agency on aging about other sources of income and whether or not your mother qualifies.

2. If your mother is able and willing, encourage her to work part-time. For example, McDonald's has a wonderful program of part-time employment for older people. (See Resources.) Visit your local fast-food chain with your mother and talk to some of the older employees if possible. There have been some cases of the younger employees making life miserable for the old people.

Other employment opportunities abound. I have met many sixty-, seventy-, and even eighty-year-old church secretaries. Recently I talked to a seventy-year-old woman who worked part-time in a supermarket. She told me that she would probably work full-time except that she was taking piano lessons and needed time for practicing. This woman was bagging groceries and wheeling them out to the customers' cars!

If your mother has office skills such as typing, word processing, filing, or even answering the phone, she could work as a temporary office worker, choosing the most convenient times.

If working part-time appeals to your mother, do some investigating for her. Job hunting is the pits at any age, but when you're old, it's terrifying. Besides the extra money your mother would earn, a job could do wonders for her morale.

If your mother decides she would like to work part-time, the first thing she must do is inventory her skills. Next narrow down what she is particularly interested in (office work, dealing with the public, working with children) and then determine where to look for a job. A job that isn't too demanding would probably be best. Make it clear to a prospective employer that this is only temporary part-time work. One sixty-plus woman went to work part-time as a typist. She was so good that within a month her boss had her enrolled in word processing. The training was very frustrating and too much for the older woman to handle, so she quit.

If your mother really wants to work, warn her that she will almost surely run into discrimination. It's against the law, but it exists. I have experienced it and it hurts.

Transportation to and from the job is one of the most important factors to consider. If your mother drives, there is no problem. Or perhaps she can consider public transportation.

If your mother was a teacher, she could tutor young people in her home. She could give art or sewing lessons.

3. If necessary, you could set up a program of giving

money to your mother that would allow her to save her pride. You *and* your siblings might contribute. Birthdays, Mother's Day, and Christmas offer great opportunities.

a. You could each send her a few dollars each month.

b. You could each save a few dollars each month and send a check at Christmas, on her birthday, or on Mother's Day.

c. Your siblings might send you a few dollars each month and you could either buy groceries for your mother or put this money into her saving account. Let your mother decide.

d. You could do as one family did: They had a "Mom's Month" once a year. They practiced an austerity program and put all the money they saved into a special account for their mother. If someone needed toothpaste during that month, for instance, they either borrowed or used baking soda.

One daughter diligently clipped cents off coupons and kept a record of the money saved and gave the money to her mother.

No mother wants donations from her family. She wants to be the one buying things for them, gifts for the grand-children. So if it becomes necessary to help your mother financially, be as discreet and gracious as possible.

Your mother probably never thought about living long enough to use up all of her money, but you and she can work this matter out together. At the same time you should know that you must start your own retirement planning long before you reach the age of sixty-five, because the odds are that you will live even longer then your mother. Help-ing her now can be a great training period for you.

Following are a few things to consider:

• No one financial plan will be adequate. Look into everything that's available.

• Your mother's money should be working for her. Keeping too much in a noninterest-bearing checking account is foolish. It's also too easy to spend too much. A good rule, if it's possible, is to keep enough in the checking account to cover at least one month's expenses. Then if a Social Security check or pension check is late or lost in the mail, bills can still be paid. Many banks offer free checking accounts to senior citizens.

• Get your financial advice from professionals, not from well-meaning relatives. Reputable financial advisers are well worth the fee they charge. When you select a financial adviser, be choosy. Check with your local Better Business Bureau. Try to get a CPA (Certified Public Accountant), because he or she is a specialist. Some financial planners are eager to help you lose your money. Fraudulent schemes abound. Check very carefully before you agree to let anyone handle your mother's money. (See Resources for specific associations to write to for advice.)

• Don't relax after everything is in order. Once a year check out changes and reevaluate. Tax laws are constantly changing.

• Saving money is not the only answer. Look at other options, such as an investment portfolio.

Inadequate funds can cause many problems. Mix these with your feelings and those of your mother and your siblings and you are in an explosive situation. If everyone works together and no one is afraid to make small sacrifices, it should be fine.

Your mother grew up during the Great Depression and during a world war and she learned a lot about going without things, even so-called necessities. She fears running out of money and becoming a burden to her children. She recalls her first job and the paycheck she and her husband lived on, and may think that what she now has in her savings account is a lot of money. You know that, because of inflation, it's very little. Determine what her financial picture really is so that she may reassure herself.

Some older people who have money and are prepared for the retirement years are helping their children by paying grandchildren's tuition or the down payment on a home. As one woman wrote, "I have every intention of living for many more years. Why should my children have to wait until they are in their sixties to get the money I'm leaving to them? They need it now!"

You also have to consider the possibility that your mother might marry again. Why not? Many older women do. Your mother may leave all of her money to this second husband. If this idea distresses you, remember, it's her life and her money. She has the right to do as she pleases with both.

One bright person suggested, "Your mother might marry a childless millionaire." In that unlikely case, neither you nor your mother will have to read this chapter.

Even though your retirement (and/or your husband's) is not in the near future, begin planning now. The Social Security Administration will give you a free personal-earnings and benefit-estimate statement. This includes estimates of future Social Security benefits. Contact your local Social Security office and ask for Form SSA-7004, or call 800-937-2000. In about six weeks after you return the completed form, you will receive a statement listing estimates of your monthly retirement benefit at ages sixty-two, sixty-five, and seventy; your survivor's monthly benefits if you (or your husband) were to die this year; and your disability benefits if you were to become disabled this year. You will also receive a summary of your past earnings.

The information on disability and survivor's benefits could save you a great deal of money in premiums by keeping you from overinsuring.

The information on your monthly retirement benefits will tell you how much you're going to need in other investments in order to maintain a certain income. Don't forget to figure on inflation. These are only estimates based on your guess of future earnings, so you should review and make adjustments every few years. Remember, one day *you* will be a caregivee.

(Turn to Resources at the back of the book for more information.)

CHAPTER 9

Safety First

As your mother's caregiver you need to make sure that her surroundings are safe. She may live in the same home she's lived in for many years, or in a new home or apartment. Things can go wrong or wear out and become hazards no matter where she lives.

In one year more than half a million people over sixty-five were treated in hospital emergency rooms for injuries suffered at home.

Every year people are hurt in accidents in the bathtub or shower, on slippery floors or stairs. They are burned on stoves. The majority of these accidents happen to older people.

Seventy percent of all people who die from clothing fires are over sixty-five.

Following is a safety checklist for your mother's home:

- Install smoke alarms and regularly check the batteries.
- Eliminate all scatter rugs (or make them skid-proof).
- Replace light bulbs with at least 60-watt bulbs. Older people need about three times as much light as young people.

• Stairs should have handrails, be covered with rubber skids or glow-in-the-dark strips, and have light switches on the adjacent walls at both the top and the bottom.

• Have a telephone and lamp on a nightstand by your mother's bed.

• Store heavy pots and pans on lower shelves.

• Keep sharp knives in a separate place away from other utensils.

• There should be handgrips bolted to the wall of the shower or bath and near the toilet.

• Place adhesive strips or a rubber-suction mat in the tub.

• There should be an emergency exit plan in case of fire.

• Keep towels and curtains away from the stove.

• The kitchen should be well-lit, with ventilation fans.

• Keep a sturdy step stool handy.

• Have the water temperature on the hot water heater set no higher than 120° F.

• Make sure all medicines are clearly labeled and that their expiration dates are checked.

• Keep electric appliances away from sources of water.

• Install an optical viewer on the front door.

• Keep electrical cords in good condition, not frayed, and not in a position to trip anyone.

• Keep emergency numbers on or near the phone.

• Install a railing on the outside steps. If your mother slipped and fell in winter, she could lie there long enough to freeze to death. Make arrangements with one of her next-door neighbors to call a doctor in case of an emergency when you can't be reached.

To obtain a free checklist, see Resources.

More than six million burglaries are committed in houses

and apartments each year. Many of the victims are older people.

Make sure your mother has security locks on all doors. If she moves to a new home or apartment, have the locks changed.

If your mother has an answering machine, taping the outgoing message using a man's voice could make her feel more secure.

Don't frighten your mother, but impress upon her the importance of protecting herself. Old people of today lived in an era where it was safe to leave your doors unlocked and to walk alone at any time of day or night. Your mother must be aware that times have changed. One mother's caregiver made sure that her mother's apartment was burglarproof. But her mother, unable to sleep one night, took a walk at 5:00 A.M. and a man followed her right into her apartment and raped her. Tell your mother not to carry ID tags on her key ring and to be extremely cautious about opening her door to anyone.

Ask the mail person to ring your mother's doorbell when delivering the mail. If she doesn't respond, the mail person can tell a designated neighbor or call you.

A few other safety measures: Check your mother's Christmas tree cord and lights. Be sure they're in good shape or a fire could result.

One elderly woman lived alone in an apartment and did very well except that she often took walks, forgot her key, and locked herself out of her apartment. If your mother is forgetful, suggest she wear her key on a chain or ribbon around her neck. Or give an extra key to a neighbor.

If it's difficult for your mother to get around, have extension phones in several rooms, or buy her a cordless phone. If she is hard of hearing, contact the AT&T Special

Needs Center (800-233-1222) for a built-in amplifier. An elderly lady wrote, "Can you imagine what it's like to be not only old but nearly deaf as well? As my hearing faded, so did my friends and even my children. They became annoyed when I didn't hear what they were saying." Not being able to hear can be a safety hazard too.

If your mother is hearing-impaired, get *The Ultimate Listening Source*, a catalog of devices that can improve her everyday life. Call 201-347-7662 to receive this catalog.

Encourage your mother to leave a hall or bathroom light on all night, particularly if she gets up in the night. It might not be easy to convince her to do this, because she belongs to the generation that was taught to turn off lights at night. Show her that it doesn't cost that much.

Examine every area of your mother's surroundings. She should have a teakettle that makes a noise, a gripper to help open bottles and jars, a kitchen timer to remind her of things cooking on the stove. Overlooking, or being careless about, the safety features of your mother's home could mean death or serious, disabling injury. Special devices can be purchased if your mother has limited mobility. Call ABLE-DATA, a national rehabilitation center in Washington (800-346-2742).

If your mother drives, suggest she look into the AARP 55-Alive program. (See Resources.)

Sears, Roebuck has a catalog listing special gadgets. (See Resources.)

CHAPTER 10

Nutrition and Health

One day an elderly woman was shopping with her caregiving daughter. She leaned over a counter, suddenly turned pale, and nearly fainted.

Her daughter was alarmed and wanted to take her to a doctor.

"Oh, no," her mother protested. "That was just a little fainty spell. I'll eat a piece of cheese and I'll be okay."

A few days later the daughter told one of her mother's friends about the incident, and the friend said, "I'm not surprised. That's happened before and I think I know why. Your mother doesn't eat properly. I have spent days with her and she snacks on cookies and candy and potato chips all day."

The daughter got her mother to a doctor and was devastated to learn that her mother was suffering from malnutrition.

"The homeless, street people, bag ladies, the poverty-stricken suffer from malnutrition," the daughter thought, "but not my mom!"

Far too many elderly people consume too little of the

essential foods, and physical and mental deterioration in many is due to poor eating habits.

In many cases senility is a direct result of malnutrition. So is osteoporosis. Maturity-onset diabetes is common and can be linked to an improper diet. Other diseases that were once blamed on the aging process are now known to be the result of malnutrition.

Why does this happen? Your mother has been aware of the importance of a proper diet for many years. She is the one who made you eat your veggies, drink your milk, and cut down on sweets. One reason is she has no one to cook for anymore. Eating alone is boring and it's too much trouble to peel and pare and slice and cook for one. Mealtimes can be any time she gets hungry. Your mother's sense of smell has lessened, which is linked to her sense of taste. Some foods are too difficult to chew, and gradually she just gives up.

It's not difficult to understand. If, day after endless day, you prepare meals, sit alone at a table or in front of the TV, and eat, it doesn't matter what you eat. You don't care. For so many years mealtimes were happy occasions, often the only times during the day when the whole family was together. Your mother enjoyed cooking and baking for the family, and she paid attention to minerals and vitamins so that her family would be healthy. Now she has only herself to think about. Also, depression may cause her to lose her appetite.

What can you, your mother's caregiver, do about her waning interest in food? You can't teach her about proper nutrition. She already knows what a proper diet is; she simply doesn't care. You can periodically check on her eating habits. You want to help make your mother's life as pleasant as possible and worry-free as possible, and one of the easiest ways is to see to it that she eats properly. Let her doctor determine if she needs a vitamin or mineral supplement. You can have Meals On Wheels delivered to your mother once a day. Many who deliver these meals also take time to talk to the elderly people. If you explain to them that your mother doesn't eat properly, the person delivering the meals can encourage her to finish her meal.

When you and your mother go grocery shopping, read labels. Ingredients are listed in descending order according to weight. If a product has a high sodium or calorie content or contains palm or coconut oil, don't buy it. We are seeing more "lite" foods now with no preservatives and low-sodium content. Check the ingredients listed on the labels of these so-called "lite" foods too. "Lite" doesn't always mean light.

Your mother needs nourishment from each of the basic four food groups every day:

1. Fruits and vegetables
2. Whole-grain and enriched bread, cereal, rice, pasta
3. Fish, poultry, meat, eggs, dried peas and beans
4. Milk, cheese, dairy products

I am far from being an expert on nutrition, but I have read many books on the subject, just as you can. As a result I eat fish and poultry almost exclusively, as well as frozen or fresh vegetables. I allow myself bacon once a year; I never eat sausage, canned soup, cured ham, hot dogs, or lunch meat. I have thrown away my salt shaker. I seldom eat sweets and I make delicious omelets out of egg whites and green pepper, onion, and mushrooms, French toast made with egg whites is great. I have followed this diet for nearly fifteen years and I truly believe it's one of the main reasons why I am enjoying my old age. Also I take virtually no medication. A nurse told me some years ago that she was convinced that old people who enjoy an excellent quality of life are not on medication of any kind. There will be exceptions, of course, but if your mother pops a pill for every minor ache and pain, or takes Valium, do everything you can to stop her.

I will admit that, in order to avoid feeling like a martyr, I order anything I want when I eat out. I usually prefer chicken, vegetables, and salad. However, if someone wants to treat me to a steak and french fries, or a piece of birthday cake, I go for it.

Six glasses of water a day are essential. I know a woman who lines six glasses on her kitchen counter every morning as a reminder. When you visit your mother, have a glass of water together instead of coffee or a Coke.

Raw cabbage has been called the body's vacuum cleaner. I mix shredded cabbage and carrots with lemon or lime sugar-free Jell-O and eat some every day. You could prepare this for your mother once a week.

Check your mother's refrigerator for leftovers. If they look moldy or have an odor, throw them away. The elderly have a tendency to save leftovers and heat them up for meals. It's easy for a dish to get shoved to the back of the refrigerator and forgotten. When you consider that one meat loaf, or one recipe for stew, can provide at least five or six meals for one person, you'll see that refrigerating leftovers is not always a good idea. A better idea is to immediately freeze the food in small portions. If your mother doesn't have a microwave oven, buy one for her. Show her how to use it. When you make nutritious meals for your family, freeze a small portion for your mother. Buy her a cookbook with recipes that serve two.

Tell your mother you understand her lack of interest in cooking and eating but that you want to help her have a better diet. Don't nag, or treat her like a child. Instead make learning more about proper nutrition a joint venture in which both of you change your eating habits. For more information on dietary guidelines, see Resources.

Besides proper nutrition there are other health concerns:

Be alert to warning signals. Frequent phone calls from your mother and at odd hours of the day; monosyllabic responses; and casual mentions of a fall may be hints of depression or indication of a small stroke or failing mental powers.

One eighty-year-old woman simply forgot to pay her rent for three months and was going to be evicted. Her caregiver talked to the apartment manager and arranged for someone to come to her mother's apartment each month to collect the rent.

The toenails of many elderly people become thick and hard to cut. Also, for some it becomes almost impossible to lean down and do the job. Arthritis renders a formerly easy task difficult. Letting them go could lead to painful ingrown nails, which would require surgery. Soak your mother's feet in soapy water to soften the nails, then trim straight across. Soothe with lotion. This will be most appreciated by your mother (she would never in a million years ask you to do this) and it should give you a very good feeling—like the biblical foot washer, symbolic of love. I talked to two young women about this. One said, "Oh, what a lovely idea!" The other said, "Ugh! Gross! I wouldn't want to do that. I'd pay for a pedicure instead."

Your mother needs regular exercise. If she is sedentary, you can suggest walks together, perhaps buy an exercise bike or a treadmill, or enroll her in an exercise class. If she rejects all of these ideas, including a daily, twenty-minute workout at home, try to convince her of the value of deep breathing. She can stand, or sit with back straight, raise her arms and inhale as deeply as possible, then exhale through her open mouth. She can do these simple exercises during every commercial on TV, while she's waiting for a pot to boil, and so on.

Suggest following TV exercise shows. Investigate the marvelous videotapes exclusively for older people.

Your mother may have some detrimental habits and she should be encouraged (not nagged) to give them up. If she smokes, encourage her to quit. Be supportive, not critical. She knows she should quit, and she knows why; maybe all she needs is a little support. Some elderly snack on candy all day. If your mother does, introduce her to more healthful snacks. This probably won't be easy. Your mother is likely to feel that you're being bossy and interfering in her life and she will probably balk.

There was a period in my young life when I thought staying out late was proof of my newly gained adulthood. My mother got on my case and constantly pestered me. So of course I stayed out late long after it had ceased to be fun. Don't nag! It only brings resentment.

In general realize the importance of preventive medicine. Make sure your mother has regular checkups by a doctor and a dentist. Ask her, on a regular basis, how she's feeling, if she is sleeping well. Listen to her. Keeping a watch on your mother's health and well-being will make a very big difference in her life.

Since I am concentrating on the emotional aspects of caregiving, this chapter on health and nutrition isn't as thorough as it could be. Still, this is such an important part of your caregiving, I urge you to read as much as you can on the subject. See Resources for suggested further reading.

CHAPTER 11

If Your Mother
Falls in Love

You might prefer not to think about the likelihood of your mother falling in love. It's possible that she will meet a man, date for a while, and decide to marry. Of course this could be a very happy development as far as you're concerned.

Perhaps, because of Social Security and other financial reasons, your mother will decide to move in with the man with whom she has fallen in love. Or she will invite him to move in with her.

Your mother could fall in love with a man who is obviously interested only in divesting her of every cent she owns. Or she might fall in love with a perfectly respectable, financially sound man whom you hate; he harbors very little love for you too. Maybe your mother will start dating a much younger man—to your embarrassment.

Any of these things could happen while you're your mother's caregiver. What can you do about it? Very little. The minute your mother marries, or a man moves in, you have lost your job as a caregiver. Depending on the circumstances, this could please you very much.

The first thing you have to do is to understand your

mother's point of view. There are three unmarried women aged fifty and over for each unmarried male. If your mother is in a romantic mood, her options are limited. If she does find someone, it's quite a coup.

An eighty-four-year-old widow wrote, "A very nice elderly gentleman asked me to marry him. I was ready, but I told him I had to have a few days to pray about it. While I was praying, another old lady came along and nabbed him!"

No matter what your mother decides to do, it's her life and her business. Still, as her daughter and caregiver perhaps you can help her toward the wisest decision.

If your mother is planning to marry, talk to her tactfully about her reasons. Don't interrogate her as if you're *her* mother. Is it because she's so lonely? Loneliness does some strange things to people. Ask her if she's sure she wants the presence of a man in her life and home twenty-four hours a day. There is nothing wrong with craving male companionship, but it should be for the right reasons.

It's doubtful that your mother will be swept off her feet with passion, at least not to the point of foolishness, but a few questions might be in order.

If your mother admits that she is marrying partly to ease her financial burden, talk to her about her assets. (When written down, they nearly always add up to more than realized.) Is there an alternative? Perhaps if your mother's financial picture is brighter, she will reconsider marriage. Maybe not, but she should consider all angles.

If your mother decides to marry, suggest that she ask a lawyer about a prenuptial agreement. She may want to see a lawyer to draw up a new will and make arrangements for estate benefits to be divided among her children and her new husband.

Remind your mother that she is entitled to know exactly what his financial situation is. If they want to, they can draw up a separate property agreement to establish ownership of everything each brings to the marriage. Your mother should be aware of her options, and you can be a big help to her in bringing them to her attention. Whether or not she takes advantage of any of them is her business.

If your mother falls in love with a man you believe is only after her money, there might not be much you can do other than stay alert, ask questions, and try to help your mother see the truth. Your mother has choices to make and you can try to guide her toward the right ones.

One caregiver's mother was being courted by a man forty years her junior. He was lazy and saw an easy life for himself. Although the caregiving daughter did everything she could to make her mother see the truth, it did no good. The young man would undo all her efforts with a bouquet of flowers or a box of candy. He was a freeloader, the marriage broke the daughter's heart, but the strange thing was, the mother was happy to her dying day.

If your mother falls in love with a man you hate, the only thing you can do is be glad your mother is happy. You will have to wrestle with your own emotions. Your main goal should be to ensure that the marriage doesn't adversely affect your relationship with your mother. Stay close to her, but not so close that you interfere with her time with her husband. Your mother will understand your feelings and be sympathetic. Many a mother has suffered because her son-in-law didn't like her. The smart ones accepted the reality but never allowed it to color the mother-daughter relationship. Eventually you may even discover that her new husband isn't so terrible after all. However, whether you like him or not, be supportive of the marriage and don't regard it as an act of disloyalty on your mother's part toward your father.

You have always been proud that your mother has stayed slim, trim, active, and attractive. Now she's living with a man much younger, maybe even younger than you. Welcome to the nineties! There isn't anything you can do but accept it. Whether the man is old or young, it's her life. You are not the keeper of her morals.

In all of these situations you as caregiver don't have many choices. Your mother is entitled to live her life as she pleases, even if it doesn't please you. Talk to her, make suggestions, help her if she asks you to, but above all let her know that you love her and that you support her in whatever choice she makes. You may feel that's just being a good loser, and maybe it is, but it beats being a sore loser. The main thing you have to concern yourself with is your relationship with your mother. Don't allow anyone or anything to spoil it. If your mother's choice turns out to be a happy one, you can still be a part of her life. If it turns sour, your mother will know that you are there for her to lean on. Your mother's marriage or involvement with a man may destroy all your lovely plans for the rest of her life. Dry your tears, enjoy your freedom, and pray that it goes well with your mother.

CHAPTER 12

Abuse of the Elderly

What exactly is abuse? We know that it's mistreatment or physical neglect. Elderly people lying in dirty beds, malnourished, covered with bedsores, even with cigarette burns and bruises, are victims of abuse. I am assuming that this kind of extreme abuse is not a problem with the readers of this book.

However, other kinds of abuse exist, of which you may be, or may become, guilty. These can sneak into your life. I'm referring to verbal abuse, psychological and emotional abuse, and neglect.

Abuse always involves personal needs. There may be a motive: greed, jealousy, resentment. There may be no motive, in which case abuse is passive. The important thing is, the caregiver can certainly be an abuser, and so can the elderly. Guidelines are needed.

I recently met a woman in her fifties who was doing her mother's grocery shopping. I asked her why she didn't bring her mother to the store. "Because she drives me crazy," she replied. "She walks so slow and stops and reads labels. I'd rather do it for her."

Then, as the clerk was checking out the groceries, the woman criticized every item, saying that she didn't know why her mother was buying that and that she didn't need this. On and on went her unpleasant tirade. I'm sure it was continued when she delivered the groceries to her mother. That is verbal abuse.

I have heard women talking to their elderly mothers as though scolding naughty children. "Mother, can't you walk any faster than that?"

"I'll take you to the store, but you're keeping me from my TV show." "Eat all of your vegetables, Mom. Now, you know they're good for you." "You spilled something on your dress again. Can't you be more careful?"

The caregiver may be practicing a form of abuse by doing more for her mother than is necessary or by bending to her every whim and desire. Pampering is abusive because it robs your mother of her independence.

If your mother is dependent on you for transportation, you can isolate her to the point where she is a captive. Maybe you run errands for her and have her groceries and medicine delivered, but you never take her out of the house unless a visit to the doctor is necessary. You discourage your mother's friends from visiting her because "it might tire her." This, too, is abuse.

I wouldn't stand for this sort of thing for one cotton-picking minute, and probably your mother wouldn't either. But many do out of fear of alienating their caregiver. Then where would they be? Little by little they become worn down into a resigned acceptance.

If an elderly person becomes extremely depressed, resigned to whatever happens, and suffers a very low self-esteem, that person is likely the victim of some sort of abuse.

Perhaps your mother is despondent, so she doesn't eat, but since she lives alone, who knows? You certainly don't want to find out one day that your mother faints from lack of food.

Maybe your mother refuses to go to a doctor when she apparently needs medical attention. Or she fails to mention that she needs new glasses or a hearing aid, when it's obvious that she has difficulty seeing or hearing. Ignoring these danger signs is a form of passive abuse.

Most abuse is passive, without any particular motivation. The caregiver simply doesn't do as much as she could to make her mother's remaining years pleasant and happy. I was guilty of this kind of abuse: passive neglect. My mother was stuck in a corner with her TV a good bit of the time. She became very quiet, sort of sad, and wasn't much fun to be around. I was usually too busy to notice, and when I did, I blamed it on her age. I see this in retrospect, after her death, and I have many regrets.

Less passive is the abuse that consists of treating your mother like a child, patronizing her, talking down to her, relating her faults to others in her presence.

Not visiting her unless you have to is neglect. Most of the elderly in nursing homes are not visited by relatives, but the elderly who live alone in their own homes can suffer the same neglect.

A woman wrote, "My daughter takes me shopping every Thursday. She is always in a hurry, impatient with my slow ways, and I always get the feeling that she is relieved when she can dump me and my groceries and be on her way. I would appreciate the gift of twenty minutes of her time."

What if this is happening to you and your mother? You're on a treadmill, running here and there, trying to please so many people, and you're getting your priorities all mixed up. What can your mother do? Beg you to sit for a few minutes to talk to her? She has probably tried that and it didn't work. This kind of treatment, week in and week out, is abusive. You don't have to hit your mother to make her hurt. In fact a black eye will heal, whereas the damage inflicted by psychological abuse will never heal. It is seldom deliberate, but no less painful.

Other people may be guilty of abusing your mother in one form or another. Children in the neighborhood can be cruel to an old lady; neighbors can give her a hard time because her yard isn't as well kept as theirs; all kinds of people could be eager to divest her of some of her money. Any of these minor oppressions can be devastating, but are usually only annoyances your mother learns to deal with. If she doesn't, or can't, you can help by making a joke of it. I mean that. After trying all the obvious things, such as talking to the neighbors, if you are getting nowhere, give up. Unless they are destroying property, you can't do much about cruel children or yapping dogs or callous neighbors.

I had a problem once with several children who took a special delight in standing under my study window and yelling and screaming. When I asked them to go somewhere else, they threw mud at my door. Talking to the children did no good and talking with their parents was even less satisfying. My whole family rallied with humor. "What did the rug rats do today, Mom?" and to the children, "You had better watch out, kids. My mom has a fierce attack cat!" In time the children tired of their little game and left me alone. In some situations a sense of humor can be your mother's salvation.

The pain is almost too much to bear, however, when the abuse comes from a daughter or son. Whether the abuse is deliberate or merely a thoughtless action, the hurt remains.

At first, caregiving isn't difficult and there is little reason for abuse. But when crises pop up in your life and your mother needs more and more caregiving or you begin to take her for granted, abuse can begin. By the time you realize that you have to correct the situation, you may be so mired down that it will be extremely difficult to pull yourself out. Some kinds of abuse can become a habit: never listening to what your mother has to say; criticizing her every mistake; constantly reminding her of her age; doing things for her but never with her.

If you can't eliminate the causes of abuse, then help your mother to present a front so that others won't abuse her. Or at least not get very far. Talk it over with her so that if something happens, she will either have a plan of action or she will come to you and you can stop it. Assure her that she won't bother you by telling you about the neighborhood kids or dogs or whatever. One woman was afraid to go out to pick up her morning paper because of the dogs running loose. When her daughter learned about this, she called the newspaper, explained the situation, and arrangements were made for the carrier to put the newspaper inside her mother's screen door. As a rule, most people will cooperate with you when you explain.

If you have a relative with a history of alcohol or drug abuse, or with severe emotional problems, that person may be abusing your mother. Particularly if that relative is a son or a daughter, your mother may be too ashamed or too protective to tell you what's going on. If you see your mother once or twice a week, you may not be aware of the fact that this person spends much time at her house. Face the fact that this relative is capable of severe abuse, and that you can't be with your mother twenty-four hours a day to protect her.

Besides keeping an alert eye on your mother, look for signs of abuse:

• Does her financial situation seem to be declining? Some clues are: she stops offering to pay for lunch; she is going without things; she's buying only the cheapest cuts of meat. Sonny (or whoever) may be bleeding her.

• Does she have unexplained black-and-blue marks? Don't accept an explanation of falling or bumping into things if bruises appear more than once or twice. Sonny may be resorting to physical violence to get Mom to do what he wants her to do.

• Is the food in her cupboard and freezer disappearing too quickly?

• Are your mother's valuables (jewelry, a silver coffee service, etc.) still there? These things will bring money for drugs or booze. They may be stolen, or Sonny may be talking Mom out of them.

• Does your mother seem depressed, melancholy, anxious? She may be protecting Sonny, and the stress is taking its toll on her.

If you discover that a troubled relative is abusing your mother, you have to put an immediate stop to it.

Take your mother in your arms and tell her you know what's going on and you know how sad the situation is. Tell her you understand why she has put up with it. Don't criticize her for trying to keep it secret and don't bad-mouth Sonny. Just agree with her that it is unfortunate and that you are going to put a stop to it. She will know that you are doing the right thing and will almost surely feel greatly relieved. Then do what you have to do. It is bound to be a very unhappy time for everyone, but as your mother's caregiver you can't do less.

My friend Mary discovered that her sister had been intercepting her mother's Social Security checks, forging the signature, and cashing them. Her mother, of course, knew this but said nothing.

When the truth came out, Mary knew that her sister had committed a federal crime but she was also aware that reporting it would devastate her mother. So she took her sister aside, let her know in no uncertain terms that she was aware of the misdeeds and gave her one last chance. She made her sister promise to repay all the stolen money to their mother. Mary had little hope of the money being repaid, but she felt that she had frightened her sister enough so that she wouldn't steal any more of their mother's checks. She also had a mail slot installed in her mother's door so that the mail would not be in a box on the outside.

You're a caregiver for no reason other than your love for your mother. It is not a legal obligation. When caregiving is performed out of love, as it nearly always is, it's special. However, sometimes caregiving can be the result of a grudging sense of duty, which invites abuse. You may find it hard to believe that caregiving can directly result in the abuse of the one you love, but it can, and much more easily than you might imagine.

When you don't know what you're doing and fail to discuss the alternatives with your mother, and refuse to admit the possibility of crisis, you're out of control. Then resentment and fatigue can easily lead to abuse in one form or another.

I hope that I have shown how we can be unintentionally guilty of abuse. As with most everything in life, attitude is crucial. If you have planned your caregiving in advance, talked it over with your mother, and know how you will handle crises, you will be in control. When you're in control, your attitude will be right and you will be less apt to be abusive.

CHAPTER 13

Traps to Avoid

Traps are cleverly concealed devices set to catch unsuspecting victims. You can't avoid traps unless you know they exist. It would be wise to become aware of the following fallacies that could snare you:

• *The truth will disturb Mom and make her unhappy.* You are having problems in your job; you have quarreled with a brother or sister; your husband is complaining about the time you spend with your mother. Don't fall into the trap of believing that your mother should be shielded from these worries.

The woman is tougher than you think, and growing old hasn't made her softer. Telling her that everything is fine when it's not is dishonest. You are denying her the rights and privileges of partnership. Tell her your problems. She won't go to bed with the vapors. In fact she will probably have some very good advice. At least she'll be a sympathetic listener. Don't be surprised if she says, "Why, I had that very same problem." After all, you want to know about her problems so that you can help. So does your mother. She'll appreciate being involved in your life. By avoiding this trap you gain a deeper, richer relationship with your mother.

• *You must act swiftly in a crisis.* Your mother falls and breaks her hip. You think, okay, this is it, and begin looking for a nursing home. Stop. Your mother will be in the hospital for a while, so use that time to calm down, ask the doctor questions, find out the alternatives available. Talk it over with your mother. Don't rush into anything. It's much too difficult to reverse a decision once you have taken action.

Don't panic when you reach an impasse. Probably it isn't an impasse at all. The dictionary defines *impasse* as "a blind alley, not open at one end." Actually it's probably a barrier that you can circumvent, a trap that you can pull yourself out of or avoid in the first place.

Maybe you're crunched financially, or a helpful brother or sister moves to another state leaving you as the sole caregiver. Any number of things can cause you to panic. Foresee these situation as traps you can fall into and deal with them as calmly as possible. Tell your mother what has happened, how it has affected you, and what you're considering doing about it. Together you will find a way out.

• *Everything will go on just as it is.* You know this is not true, but often we act as though it were, and when something happens, we're surprised. Expect the unexpected. Be ready to roll with the punches. "I never dreamed Mom would fall down those stairs. I'll have a ramp constructed tomorrow." If you anticipate unwelcome change, you will be able to deal with it. If you sit up on a rosy cloud believing nothing will ever change, you're going to drop with a bang.

• *Dear, sweet Mom won't get stubborn with me.* Old people get very stubborn about certain things. Your mother's obstinacy may seem unreasonable to you—and definitely frustrating—but there isn't very much you will be able to do about it. Believing it won't happen is a trap. Perhaps your mother is living in her home and it's much too big for her and too far from your home. Your reasons for wanting her to move are sensible and practical. Her reasons for wanting to stay make little sense. ("It has always been my home. I need extra bedrooms for when the grandchildren visit. Where would I put all my things?")

Trying to force her to move would be wrong and most likely futile, but maybe you can convince her. If you are aware of this trap, you can be prepared. You can show her the financial advantages, point out how a small home will be easier to keep clean, how being close to you means she will see you more often. Take a day or two and look at smaller homes and/or apartments together. Tell her how the grandkids think rollaway beds and sleeping bags are fun. Remind her that even the most expensive, plush retirement villages do not have guest bedrooms.

Try not to get impatient with her stubbornness. She has lost so much, and the fear of losing more makes her determined.

• *Your mother's extreme independence is a threat.* Don't fight it. Work around it, help her keep it, applaud her for it. She is going to hang on to it no matter what.

Imagine how life would be if someone robbed you of your independence. The loss of your mother's independence could push her straight into the grave. She is aware that she could lose it in little pieces, here and there, and it frightens her. Be as understanding as possible.

If your mother says, "It's great that you take me to the beauty parlor once a week, but I'll get to the doctor on my own," don't argue with her. Let her do anything she wants to do on her own, even if she goes to extremes, unless she endangers herself of course. Keep reminding her that you are ready and willing to help, but let her ask. The day will come when she will have to let you do some things. In the meantime enjoy your freedom and let your mother enjoy her independence.

One elderly woman told me, "I sneak away now and then. I call a taxi and go shopping alone. I don't tell my daughter, because she would have fits."

One daughter bought a new car and said to her mother, "I won't even try to teach you how to drive this. You'd never be able to figure it out." (This to a woman who had owned quite a few cars and had driven for over thirty years!)

Remember, you are not and cannot be mother to your mother. Admire her for the independent woman she is.

• *Mom needs to have young people around her.* Some people believe that the company of young people keep the elderly young. This is not necessarily true. Sometimes young people only make old people feel older. Young people wear them out. Young people are usually too busy expounding their own ideas to listen to old people. Their behavior is natural, and certainly it's good to be with young people now and then. However, for the most part older people prefer the company of their peers, so don't get upset with your mother if she spends most of her time with old people. She's doing what she wants to do.

• *Mom needs protection from other people.* Your mother needs protection from muggers and burglars but not from all other people. One caregiver became very upset when a family moved next door to her mother. Their dog made a second home of her mother's porch, and the four-year-old girl ran in and out several times a day. Without discussing the matter with her mother, the caregiver asked the neighbors to please keep their dog and child away from her elderly mother. The mother had no idea why her newly found companions were staying away from her.

What this caregiver didn't realize was that the dog and the little girl had changed her mother's lonely days to bright ones. If only she had discussed her intentions with her mother, she would have found out that her mother enjoyed having the dog on her porch. She fed him little treats and petted him and thought of him as her friend. The little girl was a constant delight and they had developed a very special friendship. Now and then the child would pick a flower from the old lady's flower bed and present it to her. She served the child juice and cookies. When the girl stayed too long, Mom told her she had to go home. "I'm old," she said, "and old people need to take naps."

Don't worry about people imposing on your mother or taking advantage of her. If she can't handle it, she will call you for help.

• *Mom is a built-in, free baby-sitter.* Wrong. You may think that because she loves her grandchildren so much, she will always be willing to baby-sit. So often in recent times I have heard able grandmas emphatically say, "I will not baby-sit." It used to be taken for granted that Grandma would baby-sit whenever she was needed. Today most grandmas feel different. No matter how capable your mother is, how much she loves her grandchildren, don't regard her as your built-in baby-sitter. You will be disappointed and your mother may become angry.

There are several reasons: no one should be taken for granted; your mother will eventually resent it; it's not fair to assume that your time is valuable and your mother's isn't. Even if she would rather stay home in her nightgown and robe and watch TV, that time is valuable to her.

If it becomes understood that your mother does the

baby-sitting in return for your caregiving, what happens when she is no longer able to baby-sit? Does she have to feel like a charity case?

• *I don't have to be as careful and considerate with my mother as I am with others. After all, she's my mom.* It's easy to feel this way. Your mother has always taken care of you, and you forget that your roles have changed. Your mother could have hurt feelings and get darned tired of your inconsiderate ways. For example, you have promised to take your mother out to lunch. She spends the morning getting ready. (She does that. The days when she could slip into a dress, run a comb through her hair, and be ready to go are long past.) You call just before noon and say you can't make it. Your reason is less than satisfactory, but your mother says it's all right. After all, beggars can't be choosers.

You wouldn't have to do that to a friend very often before you lost that friend. Just because you're a caregiver and doing as much as you can for your mother doesn't give you permission to forget your manners.

Avoiding all of these attitudinal traps will be easier if you remember that your caregiving springs from love, not from guilt or duty.

Your mother is the only one you will ever have, and when she dies, she will take a little part of you with her. What you do and say now will dwell in your heart for as long as you live, so be aware of the traps that may cause you to say and do the wrong things that you will regret.

CHAPTER 14

Fix It Anyway

You have planned your caregiving together with your mother and as the years go by, you're reasonably satisfied that all is well. Don't become too complacent, or you may miss some problems brewing on the back burner.

In the business world a well-run organization tries to fix things before they break. It is constantly on the lookout for small, seemingly insignificant warning signs that speak of trouble down the road.

If a crisis does occur, the reaction to it is preplanned and swift in order to minimize possible damage.

Afterward the crisis is studied to determine what happened and why and who was at fault.

Caregivers should operate in a similar manner. Be alert for warning signs and try to fix it before it breaks. If it breaks, know beforehand what you will do.

Your mother may not talk to you about how her aging is affecting her. She may refuse to discuss anything concerning her death. Yet these subjects are certainly on her mind and may be distressing her. Nothing can be done about advancing age or death, but you can help by helping her bring these subjects out into the open. Talking about a fear often dissolves much of it.

I know some elderly people who absolutely refuse to discuss their old age and what might, and probably will, happen in the years to come. They become quite agitated if the subject is mentioned. A TV commercial demonstrates their sensitivity quite well. An elderly man is talking to an optometrist. He angrily asks, "Are you telling me I'm old?" The optometrist replies, "Oh, no. You're a young man. But your sixty-year-old eyes need glasses." The old man responds with a smile. "That's better."

I have seen this same anger on the faces of old men and old women. "I am not old!" they insist. When I state, "I'm an old lady," you would think I had said something dirty. The reaction is nearly always, "Don't say that! You are not old!" One dear woman wrote to me and said, "I finally got to the point where I could admit that I am old, and other old people always respond with anger."

I believe I understand their anger because I think it stems from fear. They are afraid to face the truth that they may not always be as healthy as they are now. I suspect they have vivid imaginations. They envision themselves growing old and older, humped over, shuffling along, barely able to see or hear. So of course they're afraid of old age. I don't see myself that way. I may have a touch of arthritis, or my bum knee may give me trouble, but otherwise I picture myself mellowing into a peaceful, happy old age, and I'm not afraid.

If your mother is reluctant to discuss her aging, or fights it, talk about it. Ask her what it's like to grow old; tell her about some of your fears. Present the attitude that aging is a wonderful ripening process and has its own peculiar beauty. In time your outlook should help your mother to accept what's happening to her, to be more comfortable with it. A sense of humor will help a lot. Share with her the funny jokes and stories and cartoons circulating about old age that don't make fun of the elderly but rather laugh with them. Anything you can have a good laugh over isn't so frightening.

You don't like to think about your mother's death and you're uncomfortable discussing it with her. She isn't near death, so it isn't broken, but it may need fixing. Listen to your mother. She may be dropping clues that you're not picking up. If she says something like, "When I die . . ." don't interrupt her by saying, "Oh Mom, that's a long way off. We don't have to talk about that." Instead listen. Let her tell you how she wants to die, how she feels about it.

I once said to my son, "When I die, I want . . ." He interrupted, "You're not going to die, Mom."

"I am, too."

"Not for a very, very long time."

"But some day."

"Let's not talk about something that's so far off."

He left me feeling frustrated. I think I feel better about what a young man said to me on the day I got a kitten. He looked at me, then at the kitten, and said, "The two of you will probably last for the same amount of time."

I want to discuss these things with my children. I know that all elderly women don't feel as I do, but their caregivers can gently and lovingly lead them to discussions about aging and death that should prove beneficial to both. You need to understand your mother's aging and her feelings about death. Your mother needs to stop acting ashamed of her condition so that she can communicate her needs to you. Her denial needs fixing. It's a matter of being honest with ourselves and with each other. If your mother skirts around the subject of death with phrases like "She lost her husband two years ago," respond with "I sure hope someone is looking for him." If she says, "Now, if something happens to me . . . ," ask her what she means. "Do you mean if you die?" Refusing to talk about the obvious closes doors of communication between you and your mother, and neither of you wants that.

I matter-of-factly tell my daughters about the varicose veins snaking around my ankles, about how my once thick hair is so thin, about the lines and wrinkles, all of the things that come with age. In talking and joking about them, I erase some of the anxiety. I like to believe that when the same things happen to my daughters, they will remember our talks. "Here we go," they will say, "just like Mom said," and as a result they will be able to handle their aging with honesty and less fear.

I want to talk to my children about my death. Dying is an important event, and I only get to do it once. It's also the very last thing I will do. At first the children refused to talk about it. "Don't talk about dying, Mom. That's gross." Discuss it if your mother wants to.

Since you are a pioneer caregiver, it would be a good idea to keep a journal or diary. Jot down dates, your mother's age, what you do, how things worked or why they didn't. What plans you and your mother made. How you and your mother talked about her aging and her death and how these conversations helped both of you. If you don't like to write, you could put this on tape. Your mother could keep a diary too. One day, as your children enter the caregiving years, these diaries should provide insight and understanding for them.

CHAPTER 15

Should Your Mother
Live with You?

It used to be a foregone conclusion that when Dad died Mom would move in with one of the children. Sometimes it was a happy move, sometimes it wasn't. At least back then it wasn't for a very long period of time.

Today few mothers and their caregivers are choosing this course. Neither Mom nor her children view this option as desirable. Mother has been active and independent for a long time. She is able to live alone and take care of herself with minimal caregiving. Even after she has grown much older and requires more caregiving, she can still manage to live alone.

However, if you're considering inviting your mother to move in, first ask yourself:

• Do you and your mother get along? Does she get along with your husband and children? If your reply is "We all get along fine except for Mom's stubbornness. That drives us all crazy!" think twice. Your mother is not going to change. The little things that "drive you crazy" may be more than you can handle on a daily basis over an extended period.

• Is your mother the type who will "fade into the wood-work" when necessary or will she cause your husband to bemoan his lack of privacy and make the children reluctant to bring their friends home?

• Is there enough room in your home? Besides a room for your mother, are the other rooms large enough so that when you're all in one room, you don't feel as though you're sitting in each other's laps? In the happiest arrangements, both Mother and the family respect each other's privacy. Your mother should have her own TV and/or radio in her room and her own phone. One woman wrote, "My mother lives with us, and every evening after dinner she goes to her room. This consideration of our privacy means so much."

• If your mother would have to move to another part of the country in order to live with you, will she be able to adapt to long, cold winters or no change of seasons or extreme heat and humidity? The Older Adult and Family Research and Resource Center in Menlo Park, California, says that a sizable percentage of elderly people become seriously depressed after moving to another part of the country. They make the move in order to be near grown sons and daughters. Many elderly, after making the move, find they can't adjust or make new friends or adapt to a different social environment. As a result they spend days and nights watching TV and suffering from insomnia.

A woman wrote that she had lived in a small community in Indiana for most of her life. At the urging of her daughter in California she moved there and was so miserable she wished she could die. Eventually she moved back to Indiana. I have heard from several older women who have made moves of this kind and none of them are happy. I have also heard from a few stubborn ones who refuse to uproot themselves and are happy with that decision.

• Will you and your family be able to go on living your life the way you want to whether or not your mother approves? How does your mother get along with your children? Does she overindulge them? Does she agree with your methods of discipline? Does she recognize your authority over your children?

Ann Landers received a letter from a grandma saying that if she didn't cook for her grandchildren, they wouldn't eat properly, if she didn't make the children's clothes, they would be wearing rags. If she didn't teach them manners, they would be barbarians. She went into every facet of the children's lives, concluding with the statement that she felt trapped. Obviously, she was bitter. I would be willing to bet her daughters and sons were bitter and resentful too. I don't know what gave her the idea that it was her job to raise her grandchildren, but she was way off base. If your mother has this attitude, you don't want her living with you. You probably wouldn't want her living in the same town.

We have all seen the young mother with her elderly mother and the grandchild in the store or on the street. The child does something she's not supposed to do. The mother scolds her and immediately Grandma steps in. "She didn't mean it. She won't do it again. Come to Nana, sweetheart." That and that alone is good reason for not having your mother live with you.

If it's your mother-in-law, does she always stick up for your husband? No matter what he does? She may be Militant Millie, checking to be sure you're doing right by her Sonny.

All of these are vital considerations. I have had some experience. My daughter, Marie, and her young son lived with me for a short period. I was absolutely amazed at the way she was raising this child. She was so casual! Actually she was doing a fine job, but every day I could see her doing something that I would never do or not doing something that I considered absolutely necessary. Thank goodness her stay was only for a short time, because either I would have choked to death trying to keep my mouth shut or Marie would have resented my interference.

We can take many things on a once-in-a-while basis, but not daily. Before asking your mother or mother-in-law to move in, you and your husband have to sit down and consider everything. Realize how important her attitude and yours are. Consider your motive. Will you be asking her to move in out of a sense of duty? If you are, there are going to be tensions that could make life miserable. How do your children feel about their grandmother living with them? Ask them. If they say, "Oh, yes!" and you know it's because Grandma spoils them rotten, don't pay any attention. You're smarter than your kids. Would they want to bring their friends home if Grandma lived with them? What about stereos and loud TV? What about afternoon and evening snacks? One grandmother had the job of cleaning the kitchen after the evening meal. The kids were used to getting snacks later in the evening, but now if they left so much as a crumb on the counter, Grandma was angry. A crumb or two doesn't bother you.

Most mothers don't want to live with their children. As one put it, "I'm sometimes lonely, but I enjoy my freedom and bossing myself around." I have heard from many older mothers who won't leave their homes to live near their grown children. One well-meaning son said to his mother, "Come and live with us. We want to take care of you." She answered, "Heck, I'm only eighty-four. I can take care of myself."

Take a look at your family life. Is the TV on most of the time? Are the kids noisy? Do you all enjoy having pizza delivered at least once a week? Do you and your husband argue loudly on a fairly regular basis and then kiss and make up? Do lots of visitors and friends drop in?

What if noise gives your mother a headache, she hates pizza, too many people make her nervous, and when she hears people arguing, she gets sick to her stomach?

It will be much easier for you to consider all your options and make other arrangements than it will be to change your mind once your mother has moved in.

Neither you nor your mother should act on impulse. You may both be left with the bitter ashes of discontent, arguments, and hurt feelings.

It might be a good idea to have your mother visit you for a month to see how well it goes. Try to forget that she'll be leaving at the end of the month and pretend she has moved in permanently. If you can't wait till the month is over, it would not be a good idea to consider asking her to move in. Study the reactions of your husband and children during her visit.

On the other hand, it might go very well for you and not for your mother. From your viewpoint, you have help with the household chores, you have a baby-sitter in residence, and the rent money your mother pays you is a godsend. From your mother's viewpoint, she hates all household chores and she resents having her baby-sitting taken for granted.

No matter what you or your mother's financial circumstances are, she should pay rent. She doesn't want to feel that she's a charity case, and you can figure out a way to use the money. If you don't really need the money, you can put it in a special account for the children's education. However, don't let money enter into your decision of whether or not your mother should live with you.

Another thing you will have to consider is the safety of your home. Read the chapter entitled "Safety First" and assess if your home is safe enough, or can be made safe enough, for your mother.

Can both you and your mother tone down your expectations? Can you both be more lenient and forgiving? Living together may reveal some secrets you would just as soon remain secret. Don't forget to examine your drinking, smoking, eating habits. Will your mother abide by your house rules?

A plus in favor of the move would be if you think your mother can be outwardly neutral and if she has friends and interests of her own.

Is there a sibling or other relative your mother could visit once or twice a year? You will surely welcome a rest from each other.

There can be a marvelous bonus or two: If your mother's eyesight is failing, you can read to her. I remember such happy hours reading *A Tale of Two Cities* to my mother. One hand held the book and with the other I rubbed her back. Books on cassette tapes are available, but when possible, read to her.

There can be more bonuses if you and your mother handle it right. One woman and her mother set aside a time each day to talk about the past. While a tape recorder recorded the conversations, the woman asked questions and her mother reminisced about her childhood, about relatives, about her marriage proposal and her wedding day. Later the daughter typed all of the memories into a book, which she had duplicated and distributed to family members.

Another advantage of having your mother live with you

is that you will have time to strengthen your special bond, to understand each other in a deeper way. One woman wrote that her children visited her but that they were always in a hurry, with one eye on the clock. "Oh, what I wouldn't give" she wrote, "for them to give me just a few minutes of their time. If we could sit back and really talk to each other. But they're too busy."

You and your mother could have sharing times throughout the day. I remember still the times when my mom and I did the dishes together. She washed and I dried and we had some wonderful conversations. Simply being together, in silence perhaps, with Mom sewing while you read, strengthens the mother-daughter bond and is something you will remember for many years.

If your mother's hearing is failing, that's a double whammy, since deafness isolates her. Living with a hard-of-hearing person can be hell for everyone. Hearing aids are available, and you can consider writing notes instead of yelling at each other. Closed-caption service for TV is an option. Perhaps both of you could learn to sign.

It is possible that your mother may become so mentally or physically impaired that she requires constant supervision and care. In that case you will probably decide to move her into a nursing home. One woman wrote, "Mom was living with us and it was fine until she fell and broke her hip. She never recovered, and we had to put her into a nursing home."

Another: "When my mother started forgetting to turn the stove off, and letting the water in the tub run over, we decided to put her into a nursing home. We did it for our family's and Mom's safety and also for our peace of mind."

It can be upsetting to the whole family if your mother doesn't have enough to do, because it makes them feel guilty.

With too much idle time on her hands, your mother will be tempted to interfere with family business. Try to encourage your mother to start a hobby. One woman makes pictures out of canceled stamps, another makes stationery out of bits of lace and sequins. You and your mother might have fun tracking down a hobby that she would enjoy. Everyone will be happier if she has interests other than sitting in her room watching TV. Nowadays opportunities abound for older people to get involved, have fun, learn, share their experiences, and do for others. Adult education classes at local universities are usually offered free to people over sixty-five; senior citizen centers have varied activities. The public library has book discussion groups and will help her get started on a literacy program: teaching other adults to read.

Perhaps your mother is interested in becoming a mentor to a young person. Most communities sponsor such programs. Local schools use volunteers as tutors or mentors. Public libraries look for people to read to children. (See Resources.)

Don't be surprised if your mother is a little timid about joining these activities. It's one thing to say call this number, contact these people, or join this group. It may be difficult for your mother to take the initiative, particularly if she hasn't been involved in group activity. There may be several things she would enjoy, but she won't take the first step. You can help by finding out what's available and where and when and letting your mother choose those that appeal to her. Then make a phone call, set up a date or appointment, and go with her to the first meeting. Your initiative will get her started, then she's on her own. Also, you will know firsthand what the activity is all about.

Besides this, you can help your mother retain her sense of usefulness and self-esteem. Let her know that you rely on her for certain contributions to the family life. It may be keeping the cookie jar filled, or watering the plants, doing the family mending, helping the children with their home-work, making sure the family pet has fresh food and water each day. She can dust the furniture or keep all the mirrors in the house sparkling or sweep the front porch. Your mother could probably handle any number of these tasks. Let her do these things and also tell her how much you appreciate her help.

One mother saved the newspapers. She rolled them into tight logs, tied them with string, and then soaked them in water. These were stacked in the garage to dry. All winter the family enjoyed the fireplace without buying much wood.

The most important thing is not to let her feel that she's a burden. Don't do anything for her that she can do for herself. I was afraid to ask my mom to do anything. After all, she was old and I felt it wouldn't be fair to ask her to help around the house. That was a big mistake. One day I called her from work and said that I had forgotten to take meat out of the freezer for dinner. She said, "Do you mean you actually expect me to do that?"

"If you don't mind."

"You don't expect me to put it in the oven, too, do you?"

I suddenly realized what her sarcasm meant and that it was deserved. I had relegated her to a corner with no active, needed role in our life. "Would you make pot roast, Mom?" I asked. "Like you used to when I was a kid?"

It was sad to see how happy she was to be asked to be of use.

If you and your mother, along with your husband and children, believe having your mother live with you will work, then go for it. If your mother has known a few years of loneliness, the move may be wonderful for her. You and your mother can bond in a very special way and your mother's last years can be loving and happy. Your children will benefit greatly from having Grandma be a part of their lives. As one woman, who grew up in a multigenerational home, wrote, "I can't imagine what my life would have been like without my beloved Nana living with us. She made life richer for all of us."

CHAPTER 16

Family Fallout

Once the caregiving years begin, new problems or old ones that have been dormant for years can erupt.

Old jealousies can certainly arise when one person takes over the caregiving. ("Mom always did like you best. No wonder, the way you kowtow to her.")

Long before your mother dies, there can be arguments over who gets what. ("I helped Mom pick out that table and I should get it.")

You feel that God has forgiven you for the stupid blunder you made years ago, and Mom has forgiven you, but your brother hasn't. In fact he says he never will.

Part of the reason for these kinds of flare-ups is the fact that Dad is dead, Mother has become more dependent on her children, and these changes bring the family face-to-face. Hurts, angers, and jealousies are suddenly remembered.

You and your siblings may say that it isn't worth the trouble to patch things up, and maybe it isn't, except for one person: your mother. Surely this infighting among her children is breaking her heart and making her last years less than ideal. As your mother's principal caregiver, you should try to do some mending and healing. You may not succeed, but the important thing will be that you tried. ("God sets the solitary in families; he brings out those which are bound with chains; but the rebellious dwell in a dry land." Psalms 68:6)

Talk it over with your mother. Tell her what you want to do and why. Ask her to help.

Ask the jealous sister for help. Include her in as much of the caregiving role as you can. Let her know that you appreciate anything she does.

Ask your siblings to tell mother which of her belongings are special to them. They can have a long, loving conversation. If they live far away, they can write their feelings. Then help your mother change her will, or write names on labels or adhesive strips and attach them to the undersides or backs of pieces of furniture or objects.

You can ask for forgiveness for a past blunder. If it's forthcoming, healing begins. If it isn't, it doesn't matter, because what does matter is the fact that you asked. It's extremely important that you forgive yourself.

When you talk to your siblings about problems, remind them that Mom won't be around forever. Once she dies, they won't get a second chance.

Cain and Abel fought to the point of murder, and sibling rivalry has existed ever since. Nursing grudges, resentment, and unforgiveness harms your well-being and that of the entire family unit.

If only one member is causing the rift, ask other family members to gang up and help you. A clergyperson or a relative or friend may be successful at intervention.

Do whatever you can to make repairs and facilitate emotional healing. If nothing works, forget it. The fact that you tried will be appreciated by your mother. It will also give you peace of mind.

CHAPTER 17

The Pseudocaregiver

You take your mother grocery shopping once a week and call her every night. You fix things in her home when they need fixing. You take her to the doctor and out to lunch. You are her caregiver because you love her. You want to make her last years peaceful and happy and you also want to enjoy her company during these last years she is with you.

All true. But your brother is making your blood pressure rise. He never does anything for Mom, but now and then (when it's convenient for him, you figure) he pops in with flowers and a big smile. "I'm here to take my favorite lady out to dinner." What really ticks you off is the way your mother responds. Her eyes sparkle, she gets all dressed up, maybe for the first time in weeks.

Afterward the dinner is all your mother can talk about. Oh, the wonderful restaurant and the food and the service and they even went to a movie afterward. She calls her friends with all the details, she tells you over and over how Sonny insisted she have the most expensive item on the menu. You listen to her as you unclog her kitchen sink and take out the garbage.

Or maybe your sister lives on the other side of the world. She always does twice as much as you on Mom's birthday and Christmas and Mother's Day. You can understand: She's trying to make up for not being there. It's the stuff she does in-between that riles you. A huge bouquet of flowers delivered to your mother's door for no reason than simply to say, "I love you." Things like that.

It might be a good idea to get it out of your system all by yourself. Pound a pillow to death; take a lonely walk on the beach and feel the wind pushing at you. Push back. Whatever lowers your blood pressure. Then do some sensible thinking about this. Your brother and sister are not your mother's caregivers, you are. You do all the everyday things she needs, you are there for her all the time, and when Sonny and Sis do something extravagant for her, you start feeling sorry for yourself. Watch out! You're on the road to martyrdom. Hey, don't you like a little of the wine and roses in your life? Your mother does too.

You may think (and you may be right) that Sonny and Sis do these things to establish themselves in Mom's affections, or to look good to others, or to be sure they are included in the inheritance, such as it is. So what? You're the meat and potatoes, they are the wine and roses, but your mother is no dummy. She enjoys the lavish attention and knows exactly what is going on.

You are something like the director of a play. Your goal is to have everyone play their part, as you play yours, so that the finished product will be pleasing.

It might be wise to share your feelings with your mother. Tell her that you're aware of how happy Sonny's attention and Sis's gifts make her. Let her know that you're glad for her, but that you're also illogically jealous. Come right out and ask her if the mundane things you do for her are enough. Let her know that you need to know the truth. This conversation should ease your mind and set things straight.

Let your acceptance of the pseudo, part-time caregivers be your gift to your mother.

CHAPTER 18

The Absentee Sibling

If you have a sister or brother who lives on the other side of the country, that sibling should be included in your mother's caregiving as much as possible.

Your sister is not about to divorce her husband and abandon her children to move close to Mom, but she can still help in the caregiving.

Perhaps she's the oldest in the family and left home years ago when your mother was still in the mainstream, raising you and your other siblings. Much has happened to your sister during the last decade or so. Her marriage has thrived, she has children. She has put down roots in the community where she lives. Or she's divorced but has put down roots. Meanwhile your mother is no longer an active fifty-year-old with a supportive and loving husband, but is a sixty-plus-year-old widow.

How can this absentee daughter be any kind of a caregiver? You can help by keeping her informed of your mother's progress and well-being and what you're doing to assist her. Don't resent your sister or feel possessive toward your mother because you're doing all the caregiving. Don't shut your sister out. Chances are she wants to be part of Mom's caring team. Even though many miles separate them, she doesn't want to be isolated from her mother during her remaining years and one day get a phone call informing her that her mother is dead.

The absentee sibling doesn't have to feel guilty. Include him or her in your plans. Encourage them to do as much for Mom as they can and open the door for their help. Suggest things for them to do, things you know your mother would particularly appreciate.

One son shows up on a fairly regular basis and washes all the windows of his mother's house. She follows him from window to window and they chat. He can only do this about every other month, but his mother looks forward to his visits.

The absentee siblings can write to Mom on a regular basis. Old people love to get mail. They can send snapshots of themselves and their children, get their children to write to her.

One caregiver had a lot of siblings scattered all over the country. She wrote to each of them asking them to write an essay entitled "My Fondest Memories of My Childhood." When she received all of these, she put them together in a book, along with a baby picture and an adult picture of each of Mom's children. Her mother was delighted with this very special gift.

How often has your mother said to her children, "I did the best I could. I loved you and you knew that."

Now the absentee son and daughter can say to their mother, "I am doing the best I can." (If they aren't, they can just go ahead and feel guilty.)

As suggested earlier, all of your siblings can share in helping your mother financially if it's needed. Many older women don't require financial assistance, and even if they do, money alone won't make them feel loved. Also, sending money won't alleviate the absentee's guilt of not being involved. There are many ways of expressing love and it shouldn't be difficult to think of a few. If the sibling really cares enough, he or she will find ways. If they don't care enough, a list of one thousand suggestions would be futile.

It won't be too difficult keeping your mother happy. Just knowing that your siblings are trying to express their love will be enough. And she will know that you are cooperating with them and that will please her. My daughter Marie lives far from me, and when she calls and says, "Mom, I really do love you. I think about you a lot," I forgive her on the spot for not having written for so long. She makes me feel connected, in love, to her and to her family. Once in a while Marie will say, "Oh, Mom, I wish we lived closer to each other. If only I could call and say I'll pick you up and we'll go out for lunch. Wouldn't that be great?"

Yes, that would be great. But we can't. How often, when the children were little, did I say, "Oh, if only I could do this . . . or that . . . for them." But I couldn't, so I do understand Marie's feelings.

As your mother's primary caregiver, one of the things you do for her is to invite her long-distance children to be a part of the caregiving team. That way all of you are connected in love.

CHAPTER 19

If It's Your
Mother-in-law

Nearly 60 percent of all marriages suffer some degree of tension caused by stress between wife and mother-in-law.

Mothers-in-law exhibit four traits that tend to drive daughters-in-law crazy:

• She is always right there with criticism and advice on how you can do better in almost everything. Even the smallest issue can turn into a struggle over who knows more and who is in control.

Hang on to your sense of humor. Be firm and loving but stand up for yourself. Don't disagree. Tell her that you hear her concerns and will consider her advice. You may also have to tell her that the two of you can get along best if you both ease up on the criticism and advice. Be assertive. You have the right. Aggressive behavior can explode into arguments and name-calling. Being assertive is simply knowing your rights and not being afraid to stand up for them.

• She knows best what her Sonny likes. She raised him, you didn't.

Ridiculous. She knew Sonny as a child, you know him as a man. Maybe he did love oatmeal and toast for breakfast

all his growing years, but now he prefers coffee and a dough-
nut. Unfortunately every mother-in-law/daughter-in-law relationship has a built-in element of rivalry. Some mothers
find it almost impossible to let go of their sons. Your
mother-in-law is never going to allow you to be the only
influential woman in your husband's life. Why not let
her and your husband enjoy the mother-son relationship
up to a point? The boundaries are set by you, even if you
have to haul out the Bible and remind them both what Gene-
sis 2:24 says: "Therefore shall a man leave his father and
mother, and shall cleave unto his wife; and they shall be
one flesh."

• She needs a friend. The widowed or divorced, aging,
and dependent mother-in-law can present a huge problem.
She may want you to act as her daughter or her pal.

If you can assume this role and want to, fine. If you
don't want to, remind yourself that you don't have to. Explain your feelings to your husband and be firm but gentle
with your mother-in-law. ("It's not that I wouldn't like to
go shopping and out for lunch with you, it's just that I must
ration my time. I hope you understand.")

Of course she's the mother of your husband and you do
have an obligation toward her. Perhaps there is no other
relative who can, or will, be her caregiver. If your husband
is working full-time and you're not, the job falls to you. If
both you and your husband have full-time jobs, then you
will have to divide the caregiving chores. You may think
you can't be a friend to your mother-in-law, but I have
known several women who started out hating their mothers-
in-law who now love them very much. Keep this in mind.
As you both grow older and mellow out, you may discover
that you like each other after all.

• She loves to bring you gifts.

This sounds okay on the surface, but does her generosity come with strings attached? If it does, they are *her* strings, not yours. Accept her gifts graciously, with sincere thanks and let that be the end of it.

Your mother-in-law is the other woman in your husband's life. It's up to you to let an overbearing mother-in-law know that you respect her and that you expect her respect in return. You each have a unique position in your husband's life. Don't expect your husband to speak up for you. He is between a rock and a hard place. Handle the situation with dignity and with love.

One wife felt that she was doing all the running and work of caregiving for her husband's mother while he was just indulging his mother. For example the mother-in-law would call her daughter-in-law and say, "When we went shopping the other day, I told you to remind me to buy white thread. You forgot and now I need the thread."

The daughter-in-law handled it quite well. "I'm really sorry. I'll make a note of it and make sure we get the thread next week."

That evening the mother-in-law called and spoke to her son. Immediately after the phone call he hopped into his car and drove across town to deliver a spool of thread to his mother. His obedience infuriated the daughter-in-law, but her husband said it was the least he could do for the old lady.

The day came when the daughter-in-law, running errands all day, made a big mistake. She had to take her mother-in-law to the doctor, drop off her husband's dry cleaning, take their dog to the vet, and then take her mother-in-law shopping. Somehow, in all the rush, she dropped off a sample of the dog's urine at her mother-in-law's doctor and was later accused of doing it on purpose. The couple finally went to a marriage counselor.

Because the husband worked full-time and could seldom share in caregiving, he was happy to run out and buy a spool of thread for his mother. His wife should have accepted his action, which was perfectly okay and not a criticism of her. The wife was also right in refusing to get the thread. When she was accused of taking the dog's urine sample to her mother-in-law's doctor on purpose, she should have laughed it off as the funny incident it was. There has to be give-and-take on the parts of all three people involved. Nothing ever comes out exactly even. The daughter-in-law must do what is necessary to care for her mother-in-law and not resent what her husband manages to do for his mother. The mother-in-law should be reasonable and undemanding and not try to play her son against his wife. Mother should get in the habit of counting her blessings.

Encourage your mother-in-law to discuss her feelings about herself at this stage of her life. Is she bitter? Is she frightened at the prospect of having to depend on you? Are you and your husband her only caregivers? Urge her to tell you about her childhood, your husband's childhood, her marriage, her memories. "My mother did . . . did you do that, too?"

The more she can open up, the better she will feel and the closer to you she will become. The more she reveals about herself, the easier it may be for you to recognize that she is neither good nor evil, simply human. And she is your husband's mother. There is no reason to assume up front that your relationship with your mother-in-law can't be very good. There are women who get along much better with their husband's mother than they do with their own. If you can begin by assuming that you will get along, you probably will. She gave birth to and raised the man you love. That gives her an edge, doesn't it? How well you get along depends greatly on both of your personalities, but don't assume that, because she's your mother-in-law, you're rivals.

Caregiving for both your mother and your husband's mother takes some expert juggling. It also requires tact, a sense of fairness, and a generous smattering of wisdom. If you enjoy being with your mother more than with your mother-in-law, jealousy may raise its ugly head. If you enjoy being with your mother-in-law most, jealousy will surely rise up. Don't play games. Do what you want to do, be honest, and let the mothers deal with the jealousy. It's their problem, not yours.

Trying to please both mothers can get sticky. A long time ago I called my mother-in-law "Mom." My mother was furious. "Call her anything you want to, but not Mom. I'm your mother and I'm the only one in this world you can call Mom." Her feelings were really hurt.

Her reaction was silly, but jealousy always is, and you will probably have to contend with that sort of thing if you're caring for both mothers. Now that I am old, I will tell you something: I understand my mother's feelings. I like my daughter's mother-in-law very much, but I would crumble into a self-pitying heap if I ever heard her call her Mama. I only hope I would have the good sense to keep my mouth shut.

Their rivalry can drive you crazy and make your caregiving for both parents less effective. You simply have to learn not to attach too much importance to the petty things they say.

If your mother says, "I heard you took Bob's mother to a movie the other day," reply, "I sure did. It was a very good movie." Then drop the subject. Don't get drawn into a conversation on why you never take your very own mother to a movie or how come you had time for that when you couldn't go shopping with your flesh-and-blood mother last week.

Don't allow either of the mothers to come between you and your husband. If your mother-in-law calls your husband and complains about something you did or didn't do, you and he should have the response planned. ("Whatever she does is just fine with me, Mother. In fact we had already agreed that she would do that.")

If your mother starts complaining to you about your husband, you know what to do. Don't let her continue. "Bob and I will work that out, Mom" is enough. Remember, you don't have to be aggressive, but you must be assertive.

You can be your mother-in-law's caregiver and get along with her. Follow the same rules you follow with your mother and perform your caregiving with love. It's almost a certainty that your love will be returned. If it isn't, it's her loss.

SECTION III

Caregiver and Mother Have Special Needs

Both you and these people who are with you will surely wear yourselves out.

EXODUS 18:18

CHAPTER 20

A Special Prayer

Show or read this lovely prayer to your mother. She will enjoy it and relate to it. Perhaps a discussion of this prayer will bring you and your mother closer to understanding each other and both of your needs.

A SEVENTEENTH-CENTURY NUN'S PRAYER

Lord, Thou knowest better than I know myself that I am growing old and will someday be old. Keep me from the fatal habit of thinking I must say something on every occasion. Release me from craving to straighten out everybody's affairs. Make me thoughtful but not moody; helpful but not bossy. With my vast store of wisdom, it seems a pity not to use it all, but Thou knowest Lord that I want a few friends at the end.

Keep my mind free from the recital of endless details; give me wings to get to the point. Seal my lips on my aches and pains. They are increasing, and love of rehearsing them is becoming sweeter as the years go by. I dare not ask for grace enough to enjoy the tales of others' pains, but help me to endure them with patience.

I dare not ask for improved memory, but for a growing humility and a lesser cocksureness when my memory seems to clash with the memories of others. Teach me the glorious lesson that occasionally I may be mistaken.

Keep me reasonably sweet. I do not want to be a saint. Some of them are so hard to live with, but a sour person is one of the crowning works of the devil.

Give me the ability to see good things in unexpected places and talents in unexpected people. And give me, O Lord, the grace to tell them so. Amen!*

---

*Source unknown.

CHAPTER 21

Needs of the Caregiver

The late congressman Claude Pepper of Florida, chairman of the Subcommittee on Health and Long-term Care of the House Select Committee on Aging, recognized the fact that caregivers of the elderly are in need of help. The very structure of the American family is threatened by the full-time demands of caring for the elderly. Mr. Pepper believed that the government should provide, at the very least, respite care for the caregivers. The toll on caregivers and their families isn't counted in dollars as much as in sacrifices made and lives upset.

Caregiver: don't ignore your own needs. Since you will probably be your mother's caregiver for a long time, and since crises are unpredictable, it's a good idea to determine your current needs and strive to meet them. If you don't, you are not going to last to the finish line.

You need time for yourself on a regular basis. It's much too stressful always to be doing for someone else. You shop for your family, take your mother to the doctor and supermarket, prepare meals, serve on the PTA, serve as chauffeur for your kids, attend school functions. You absolutely must have some time alone. You can't put everyone on hold while you meditate, but you can look for spaces of time that you can use to your benefit. Instead of a quick shower in the morning, maybe you could stretch that time for a leisurely soaking bath. You could double up once a week on yours and/or your mother's grocery shopping and have the next week free.

One of your older children could drive your mother to the doctor; your husband could fix her lock or stopped-up sink on the weekend. View these moments as lifesavers and work at getting them for yourself. If you're interested in taking a class in painting or weaving or photography, go ahead and sign up. A class or special-interest club could be your relaxing time away from your mother and your family. In the business and professional world it is a recognized fact that people need time off from the job. You must recognize that need too. One day a week off isn't very much but it's essential for your physical, mental, and emotional well-being.

You also need freedom from nagging interruptions. If your mother is in the habit of picking up the phone and calling you every time something goes wrong or makes her unhappy, put a stop to it. Ask her to make a list and you'll take care of it all on your next visit. Maintain a schedule that's only partly flexible. You are going to have to adjust your schedule, make compromises, but you shouldn't let your plans fly all over the place at anyone's whim. You need to maintain the authority to decide what you will do and when you will do it. Tell your children, "My bridge club meets on Thursday. Unless you have a real emergency, please don't ask me to change my plans."

Your children should have an understanding of your caregiving role. You have always been there for them, and now they need to recognize and appreciate your additional responsibilities. Explain to them what you're doing and how important it is and how you can't do it without their support and cooperation. The more they can fend for themselves and help out at home, the more time you will have for them. This is good for your children. Recently one of my kids said to me, "You always made us be independent and do for ourselves. Now that I'm grown up and on my own, I really appreciate that training."

Talk to your mother too. When your family needs you the most, your mother should understand and fade into the background for a while. When she takes precedence, you need full cooperation and help from your family.

Your husband, children, and relatives, as well as your mother's friends can and should help you. Don't be afraid to ask for their help. As a matter of fact you probably will have to ask, and you can tell them that, even though you are your mother's principal caregiver, you want to give them the opportunity to help too. If they don't, seek help elsewhere. There are adult day centers for older people in many communities. High school and college kids are usually happy to run errands for a little money. One caregiver's husband goes to her mother's house once a month and checks to see that everything is working properly and does minor repairs. They have coffee and talk, and the mother looks forward to these visits. The husband feels that he's part of the caregiving and he stays on friendly terms with his mother-in-law. If your husband won't do something like this, or won't do anything at all, let it go. Don't allow it to be a bone of contention between you. Instead ask for his understanding when you have to do certain things for your mother and tell him that you appreciate this understanding. On the other hand, it could very well be that your husband would be pleased if you asked him to share in the caregiving. He may want to be part of the team but hesitant to interfere.

An elderly woman wrote, "I thought I was all set. My

daughter was very good to me. She took me places and called nearly every day. I guess her husband wasn't as content with the situation as we were, because he changed jobs and moved the family about as far from me as he could. I cried, my daughter cried, but there wasn't much we could do about it. I can't move to be near them because I realize now that my son-in-law is jealous of me and the attention I was getting from his wife. Maybe my daughter and I didn't handle it as well as we could, but he didn't either. Anyway, I'm alone now for the rest of my life and that's the way it is. I'm frightened, but I'll manage somehow. I always have."

Caregivers, think about this. Your mother may have this fear lurking somewhere in her mind. You can't assure her that it will never happen, because you don't know that, but if you and your husband agree on what you're doing for your mother and he doesn't harbor any feelings of jealousy or resentment, you can suggest that he stop in on your mother once in a while to talk to her, offer his help, or simply let her know that she isn't a burden. It will mean a lot to your mother and will dispel those vague fears of being abandoned.

One woman wrote, "My daughter has been married for nearly five years. They live about a twenty-minute drive from me. In those five years I have seen my son-in-law at Thanksgiving and Christmas, that's all." That woman has some fears, believe it.

In the case of your children, a very positive approach would probably be best. Instead of asking, "Will you do this for Grandma?" have a list of things the kids could do and ask them which ones they choose.

"Grandma likes to go to the library on Saturday mornings. She needs someone to drop her off at the library at nine and pick her up at ten and take her home. I want to be with your dad on Saturday mornings, so who will volunteer?"

The kids could keep Grandma's flower beds weeded, mow her lawn, wash her windows. If the kids do these things on a fairly regular basis, it will ease your load and it will also bring them into direct contact with their grandmother. You can bet that Grandma will be waiting for them with a cold drink and cookies and love. Even if you didn't want them to do the work, they should be included in the caregiving simply because of the intergenerational communication. It will make Grandma happy, and it will enrich the lives of your children.

If you have a friend (or friends) who is also the caregiver for her mother, perhaps you can work out a plan where you double up on some chores. One of you can take both mothers grocery shopping one week, leaving the other free to do as she pleases. The next week it's the other one's turn to do double duty.

In order to make sure that your needs are met, play the "What If?" game:

"What if Mom . . ."
"And I can't . . ."
"I will . . ."

For example, "*What if Mom* sprains her ankle and can't walk. *I can't* help her because we're going on vacation. *I will* make arrangements with Mary beforehand just in case."

This advance planning will take the burden off of you. Playing the "What If?" game can be very productive. One woman wrote, "Every time my family planned a trip or vacation, my mother became mysteriously ill. After she had ruined one trip and I had an angry husband and disappointed kids, I did something about it. I made arrangements with a neighbor (one my mother doesn't particularly care for) to move in with my mother until we returned from our vacation. She never had to do it because the 'threat' of it happening was enough to keep my mother well.''

Make your schedule and explain it to your mother. Let her know the times you prefer not to be interrupted. One caregiver said, "My mother calls every afternoon at four. She knows that's when I watch Oprah, but she always says, 'Oh, I'm sorry. You're watching that TV show, aren't you?' then talks for at least ten minutes. I'm lucky if I get to see half the show.'' The best thing to do is tell your mother that you won't answer the phone between four and five. Then don't answer it. If you are able to schedule some time in the day for yourself, make it very clear that you won't answer the phone or that your answering service will be on during that hour.

Of all your needs the most important is some time to yourself. Whether it's an hour here and there, an afternoon or a whole day once a week, you need it in order to rejuvenate. Caregiving today goes on for too long a time to risk burning out.

Don't neglect time alone with your husband. Set aside times exclusively for you two to be together. One caregiver told her mother, "Bob's retiring next month." Her mother's smile was like a rainbow. "Oh, wonderful! Now you'll have more time." The caregiver thought, "She's like a kid at Christmas," so she said, "Yes, Mother, we'll have extra time for each other." She let her mother know in a nice way that the extra time wasn't for her.

A caregiver wrote that she had cared for her semi-invalid mother for nineteen years. "Our lovely retirement plans were put on hold for a long time." If it's at all possible, don't let this happen. If you and your husband have planned to travel during the retirement years, try to work it out so that you can. With a little effort and probably not very much money, you can see to it that your mother is cared for while you and your husband go on your trips.

Congressman Pepper felt that the stress of caregiving is a threat to the structure of the American family. Think about this and take it seriously.

Following are a few ways to help you reduce stress:

• *Get real.* Plan ahead with realistic plans. Think with your head more than your heart. You may want to move heaven and earth for your mother, but instead you say, "This is what I can reasonably handle."

• *Take it easy.* Look at all your options. Figure out beforehand what will work over the long haul. You might find it easy to visit your mother every day now. But what if she grows to expect it (she will!) and one of your grown children returns home to live, or you get a full-time job, or your husband retires?

• *Learn to say no.* When I was a church secretary, I maintained a priority calendar. When someone wanted me to take on extra work, I directed them to my priority calendar so that they could see for themselves whether or not their request was reasonable or even possible. As your mother's caregiver, you should have a priority calendar, and three of your priorities should be time with your husband, time with your children and friends, and time for yourself. Eliminate the phrases "I have to . . ." and "I should . . ." from your vocabulary. These represent demands made on you by others. Set your own goals and priorities.

• *Be sure the price is right.* It's foolish to spend five dollars worth of energy on a ten-cent problem. Determine what's important and what's not. Your mother wants you to drop everything and rush over to her house because she thir her faucet may be leaking. Don't spend energy on that one. Tell her you'll get around to it as soon as you can.

• *Laugh it up.* How often do you laugh in a day? Probably not often. "There isn't much to laugh about," we say. We have to look for things to laugh about. It truly relieves stress. I am all alone in my apartment and find myself laughing out loud at the crazy antics of my cat as she chases a toy. My son says, "I only got a B on my exam," and I reply, "Oh, wow! That's the end of the world," and we both laugh. Laughter is healing, so look for something to laugh about each day.

• *Share.* When you're feeling harassed or blue, talk to someone. Don't bottle it up and brood about it. Call a friend, talk to your husband. When you share these feelings, you're no longer afraid of them and their importance wanes. Go to someone and say, "I need you to listen to me."

• *Move it.* A brisk walk, aerobics, swimming, washing windows, pulling weeds, dancing with your shadow—anything active will help relieve stress. Never sit and brood and feel sorry for yourself. Get on your feet and do something physical. It works wonders.

• *Keep the faith.* Your faith in God is restorative, and the peace that is derived from reading God's word or praying is there for you always. Take a few minutes at the beginning of each day to fill yourself with this peace and strength. Remember the old admonition "Don't rush around faster than your Guardian Angel can fly!"

CHAPTER 22

Needs of the Elderly

I don't believe there is, or ever will be, a complete under-standing between the generations. I'm not sure it matters very much.

How in the world can a young person of today under-stand the elderly's thrifty ways? People of the older gener-ation were brought up to turn off the light when they left a room, to eat everything on the dinner plate, to save money, to neither a borrower nor a lender be. How can the elderly understand young people who waste energy and food, don't even think about savings accounts, and buy anything they want because "I've got the plastic"?

An older person may understand some of the young person's actions because he or she, too, was young once, but the young can't possibly know what it's like to grow old. Aging includes too many things they have never experi-enced.

No, I don't believe there is a lot of understanding be-tween the generations, but that's not so bad. The elderly don't need to be understood as much as they need to be accepted. As long as the two generations can communicate their needs to each other and respond in love, they'll get along fine.

You say, "I guess Mom really prefers staying home. Old people are like that." Why don't you ask her? Maybe she would enjoy an excursion away from home now and then but hates to ask you.

Mom thinks, "I would love to get out more, but I don't want to pester my daughter. I'm sure she doesn't want me tagging along." Why doesn't she ask? It could be she would enjoy some small trips more if her mother were along.

An elderly woman told me, "I don't talk much when I'm with the kids. They aren't interested in anything I have to say."

That lady is wrong. Young people, and particularly family members, very often want to hear what the elderly have to say. More importantly they *need* to hear what they have to say.

You have had a frustrating, busy day at work and you're tired and angry. On the way home you stop at your mother's for a short visit to see if she's okay. Because she's your mother and elderly, you hide your feelings and put on a smile. Don't you know that it would mean a lot to your mother if you just let loose? "Oh, Mom, I've had a terrible day!" and your mother will console you, almost certainly be on your side, and for a few minutes you're back in those familiar mother-daughter roles. It brings memories of a little girl running to Mom for comfort. It can be a very satisfying time for both of you. No, you're not a baby, and it doesn't happen often, but once in a while it can be a very close, sharing experience that neither of you gets anywhere else. Your husband may respond in a less soothing way.

As you're leaving, thank your mother for helping you to feel so much better. She will have a special glow for the rest of that day.

Let your mother play the role of mom. Show her that

you still value her opinion. Don't take everything away from her. Your mother needs to retain her self-esteem, and asking for her advice is an easy way to boost it.

There is another, more subtle, way of robbing your mother of self-esteem: Give the impression that practically everything you do for her is somehow a sacrifice. I have seen this in action, and truly it was painful to watch.

Instead of saying, "I picked up some sweet rolls at the bakery, Mom. How about a cup of coffee to go with them?" the sacrificing caregiver says, "The bakery was way out of my way, but I know how you love sweet rolls, so I made the trip and got them for you."

"I was glad to do that for you, Mom. Of course I couldn't get my own shopping done, but that's okay."

"If you want to go there, we'll go. I'll manage somehow to get my own chores done."

Can you imagine how this would make you feel, if time after time, every time something was done for you, it was done at the inconvenience, at the sacrifice, of the giver?

Of course, your roles have changed, but she is still your mother, and you are her child. This is basic and will never change, but many other changes are occurring, and both of you should be aware of them so that you can adapt. For example you voice an opinion and your mother doesn't agree. You raise your voice slightly and insist that you're right. Your mother says, "Look here, girl. I changed your diapers." Her retort is designed to put you in your place, but don't stand for it. Tell your mother that the diaper-changing days are long past. Remind her that you're grown up and that your roles have shifted somewhat.

I know a young woman who never confided in her mother, never asked for her opinion. At first her mother would try to talk to her about certain subjects, but the young woman always cut her off. "Oh, I'll ask my husband about that. He'll know what I should do. He's my best friend."

It didn't take long for that mother to keep quiet. She was very hurt. Of course she was happy that her daughter had a good marriage, but was it necessary to take everything away from the mother? Once a woman marries, her mother has only a small part in her daughter's life, but it's a very special part, and it's cruel to deny her even that.

At first, when faced with the fact that your mother is old and you're her caregiver, there is a tendency to treat her differently. So many daughters patronize and condescend to their mothers. Heide used to become very angry with me every time I took a cab to go to the library or shopping. I was supposed to wait until she could take me. She thought she was being good to me, while I felt that she was trying to run my life. Also, she was treating me as though I were a child. We had to talk this out and come to an understanding. You must try to make this shifting of roles an easy transition, and the best way to do it is to talk. Ask your mother how she feels about the things you do for her. "Do you want me to do this, Mom, or would you rather handle it yourself?"

Following is a list of basic needs of the elderly. Use it as a starter. Since communication is so vital, and since your mother's needs may change as time goes on, go over the list with her on different occasions. These are very simple, basic needs. The ones your mother adds will probably be easy to meet too. If they're not, ask her how you can fulfill them. Discussing this list together will add an intimate dimension to your caregiving. In the long run it will make it much easier on you and more pleasant for your mother.

The elderly mother's needs include the following:

- *To be needed by someone for something.* Your mother has a lot of skills and she would enjoy using them. One of her biggest losses is to not be needed anymore. A woman I know rode horses most of her life but could no longer ride after she injured her back. Her very wise caregiver arranged for her to teach a group of small children how to ride.

Ask your mother to do something for you. One mother wrote, "My daughter makes cookies and brings some to me every Friday. She tells me she doesn't want me doing any baking. I don't want her cookies! I would rather be baking them for her and her family."

Tell your mother, "I'm dying for some of your bran muffins, Mom," or "If I cut flowers from the garden, would you make an arrangement for the table?"

- *To have a little fun now and then.* Living alone and being retired can become monotonous. One day melts into the next. Often your mother has to check the newspaper or a calendar to be sure what day of the week it is. Eating out, going to a movie or to the park—any excursion now and then breaks the routine. New diversions don't have to be in the company of you the caregiver. You can make arrangements for her to have a little fun now and then with other people. Encourage her to look into opportunities in your community. Most have clubs and organizations for older people that meet on a regular basis for luncheons, picnics, tours, and all sorts of activities. Some of them go on cruises together or for a week or two to Europe.

One caregiver asked her seventy-two-year-old mother what she would like to do for fun. Her mother's answer was a surprise: "Find out where I can learn to dance the Texas two-step."

- *Companionship with her peers.* Most old women enjoy

being with young people, but they also dearly love talking with people their own age. They have a lot in common and they understand each other. Maybe your mother would enjoy being in the company of a man, young or old, now and then. A widow's world, with her daughter as caregiver, is usually a completely feminine world. Having a man to talk to can be a great refresher, even though your mother may not be interested in a romantic development. One woman wrote, "I was feeling sorry for myself because my sons ignored me. I am used to having men in my life. Then I took a course at our local university and made friends with some of the young male students there."

• *Pleasant surroundings.* Is your mother satisfied with her home? Would a coat of paint or new drapes lift her spirits? Ask her. If your mother lives in her own home, her needs are going to be different from those of the woman living in an apartment. One will have faucets to fix, lawn to be mowed, house repairs to be made, whereas the other will have no maintenance worries. Still, the apartment dweller might appreciate some help in redecorating.

• *Time now and then, for short periods, with children.* If there are no grandchildren, a trip to a park or zoo where there are children your mother can watch and talk to could be a delight for her. If there are grandchildren, share them. Look at your mother's face when a child approaches her. Her expression should convince you of this need. When my children were little, we visited a nursing home for the elderly. We walked into the lobby where a group of older people sat, and in an instant my children disappeared. They were hugged and fussed over and held on laps, and I felt guilty when it was time to leave.

• *Mental stimulation.* Would your mother like to take a course at a local university? These are usually free for people over sixty-five. If so, would it be too great a burden to arrange transportation to the classes? Does she have an elderly friend or neighbor who would enjoy taking a class with her? It can be in anything: ceramics, knitting, a language, just so that it's a learning experience. Your local newspaper lists several volunteer opportunities. Your mother could volunteer to help in the library for a few days a week. She could get involved in a tutoring program, teaching an adult how to read. She might enjoy working in the church office.

• *Physical exercise.* You both know that exercise is important and will help your mother remain healthy longer. But maybe she's afraid to walk outside alone, or she forgets to take a walk. Perhaps a stationary bike or a treadmill would give her incentive. Maybe arrangements could be made with several of her friends and neighbors to walk together several times a week. Joining a bird-watching group could provide exercise and learning. Most YMCAs offer swimming sessions for older persons.

• *The feeling of being connected to all of her children (and that usually includes their spouses).* Ask your mother how often Sis calls or writes. Suggest to brother that a phone call in between holidays would make Mom happy. If your siblings live a distance away and seldom get home, it would be a good idea to let them know how Mom is growing old and how things are changing. Send a snapshot now and then. It's not uncommon for a child to come home and say, "Why didn't you tell me Mom was so old?"

• *Regular contact with someone.* Probably you. This could be necessary for two reasons: to give your mother a sense of security and to make your caregiving easier. Call your mother once a day. The calls can be either brief or long, whatever pleases the two of you. These planned calls will eliminate your mother phoning you about trivial things. As long as your mother is fairly independent, these daily calls aren't so much a necessity as a loving kindness. As one woman put it, "If my daughter didn't call me every day, I'd go nuts. I could go for days on end and not hear the sound of a human voice except on TV." If, now and then, you don't call, it's okay.

• *Touching.* A hug. A kiss on the cheek. Your husband and children touch you on a daily basis, but days can go by without your mother touching or being touched by anyone. Every time you see her, give her at least one hug. When you talk, sit close and hold her hand. We know that babies can die if they are never held, never touched. From the time my daughter was very little, I have taken her face in my hands and said, "Oh, how I love that face!" It's a ritual we both still love, and I am always rewarded with a hug.

• *Discipline.* Your mother had to show you, once upon a time, that you couldn't walk all over her and get your own way just because you were young and cute. Now you must let her know that she can't walk all over you because she's old. A soft but firm response, said with a loving smile— "No, Mom, I can't do that"—will take care of it. Your mother is not stupid, and whether or not she admires your authority, stay in control.

• *Your patience.* Your mother knows, better than you do, that she is growing older. She is familiar with the aches and pains, her slow pace, her annoying habits. Be patient. Teach your children to be patient. Love is patient and kind, and you want your children to learn these qualities before they become your caregivers. They will learn best by example.

Try going about your household tasks with one hand tied behind your back, or without once bending over. How do you clean the bathroom if you can't kneel? Walk in your mother's moccasins for a while and you will be able to be more patient with her.

• *Her self-esteem.* Talk sometimes about her past, what she did as a young woman. It counts for something. "When you were a secretary (teacher, lawyer, etc.), Mom, how did you . . . ?"

Brag to others in front of her about her past successes. She truly is more than just an old lady. Perhaps she is feeling that all she is is an old lady and you can remind her of past accomplishments. For so many years your mother held the limelight. People would stop and talk to her and say, "Oh, is this your daughter?" and you were introduced. Now your mother is with you and people stop and talk to you and acknowledge your introduction of your mother. Of course your mother's proud of you, but this is a subtle shifting of roles that doesn't do much for your mother's self-esteem.

• *A peaceful life.* Silence at times that they want to nap, read a book, or simply sit on the porch is something old people greatly desire. Your mother has lived through the noise of crying babies, boisterous children, and incredibly loud teenagers. Now she wants peace and quiet, and she's entitled to it.

• *Privacy.* You may say, "Privacy? She's alone most of the time! What do you mean by privacy?" Since you're the active one, running here and there, and your mother is home alone, it could be easy to get into the habit of dropping in on her whenever it's convenient for you. This could result in a violation of her privacy. Maybe she doesn't particularly want you to know what she's doing every minute of the day.

Those are the simple, basic needs of an elderly mother. Be aware of them and try to fulfill them. As your mother grows older, her needs will grow and change. Caregiving will not become easier for you. It is very difficult and painful to watch someone you love struggling with the simplest of things.

"We don't go to the art museum anymore. It used to be one of our favorite things to do, but lately Mom can't manage those steps."

"I talk on and on about all the things happening in my life, and Mom smiles and nods her head, but I know she doesn't hear half of what I'm saying."

You observe how your mother is aging and you wonder how you will handle your own aging. "I'm fifty-one years old and just beginning to experience the onslaught of aging. My mother is eight-six, and over the last years our roles have gradually reversed. I hope and pray I don't burn out."

You are saddened by the decline of this beautiful woman who raised you and nurtured and loved you. The woman who was your rock of strength for so many years. You want to take care of her now to show her how much you love her.

Your mother is still a little surprised at the things she can no longer do. Sometimes it makes her angry. "I just can't do it, even though I want to, and I tried so hard."

You worry about her and with good reason. "My mother never leaves the house unless I'm there to help her. She fell down the front steps once, and ever since she's been afraid."

"She has to take her medicine at different times of the day and I have put little reminder notes on her refrigerator and in the bathroom, but she still forgets."

"Mom absolutely refuses to live with us. Still, I worry constantly about her being alone. I suspect she spends a good many of her days in bed."

"I know the nights are difficult for Mom. Silence hovers

and intensifies loneliness. I got her a radio and set it to an all-night station that plays soft music. I hope it helps."

It isn't easy to accept your changing roles. "It's such a strange sensation, making decisions for my mother. She is so acquiescent and grateful for my help. It gives me a kind of power over her and I hate that."

What you have done in your lifetime, you were defined by that role. When you retire and your children leave the nest, you will lose that definition. This is the scary part of retirement for most people, and it may have happened to your mother. Remember, and help her to realize, that being a nurse or whatever is not all she is or has been. Smart people say, "That's what I do, not what I am." That way the defining lines are not so strong or so confining.

First and foremost she is your mother and that's why you love and respect her. Let her know that. If she is a generous person, talk about her generosity and how it pleases you. If she has a happy disposition, tell her how her grandchildren love being with her. Concentrate on the lovely things she is,

Taking on the caregiving of an elderly mother (and perhaps a mother-in-law as well) is a challenge. If the elderly parent is complaining and demanding, you're in danger of losing all the self-esteem you have left.

You want to do your best for your mother and help her enjoy her last years. You want to build happy memories. Still, you have your own life and you don't want to become a victim. You have learned quite well how to avoid becoming anyone's victim, but what if the victimizer is your elderly mother or mother-in-law? You can't tell them to blow it out their ear. You have to learn the subtleties of caregiving.

Caregiving has become much more than relegating your

mother to a corner of your house for her few declining years or remembering to send her birthday cards or to call her now and then. The needs of the elderly have so far been pretty much ignored, but this picture is rapidly changing.

Because the elderly population is growing, we are forced to take a long look at what aging people need and how they can be helped. We have to study our former prejudices concerning old age. Only a very small percentage of the elderly are in nursing homes: the majority are in the mainstream with caregivers to help them cope. Most of the elderly live alone and need only minimal care for a very long time. What they need from their caregiving daughters is a love that alleviates loneliness, builds self-esteem, and makes the elderly person feel wanted and needed.

As long as your mother can manage on her own (and this is usually for a very long time), her needs are fairly simple. You know she gets lonely, so you visit and take her out to lunch and you call often. You know that she can't change the light bulbs in the ceiling fixtures and can't open the child-proof bottles, so you keep a check on those things. Your mother's needs will grow, and you will adapt to meet those needs. While you're striving to do the best you can for this dear person, and hoping you're doing it right, chances are that your mother thinks you're doing fine. With open communication established, she will let you know if you're not.

CHAPTER 23

Where You Stand

The following should be completed by both the caregiver and her mother. Do it separately, giving it a lot of thought. Then spend an afternoon together going over your responses. Be honest with each other. If you feel that you need more time for yourself, for instance, say so. Tell your mother why you feel this way. Together you can then work on a solution.

So often we're not truly open and honest with each other. We don't want to hurt our mother's feelings, she doesn't want to add to our burden, so both tell little white lies.

Heide used to bring me coconut cookies on a regular basis. "I know you love these, Mama." I hated them, but I didn't want to hurt her feelings, so I thanked her and accepted them. I didn't eat them. One day, finally, I said, "Where did you get the idea that I love coconut cookies?"

"I remember a long time ago you said you loved them."

"You remember wrong. I have never liked them."

"Are you kidding me?"

"Nope."

We had a good laugh over that, and from then on when

she felt like buying cookies for me, she made sure they weren't coconut. It can be as silly as that or it can be something very meaningful.

Perhaps your mother will be honest and say, "The most important lesson I've learned is never to contradict you." That should lead to a lively discussion!

The point is, this may have been bothering your mother for some time, but she has been hesitant to talk about it.

Maybe you will state, "I can't stand it when you won't tell me what you want. Every time I come over and ask you what you want or need, you tell me that you want or need nothing. And then, later, you let me know that I failed to do something. That drives me crazy!"

Talking about these things may not solve the problems, but it will clear the air and you will both be more aware of what you're doing and saying to each other.

This should not be an occasion for a fight—or even an argument—but a way of getting to know each other better. It's a way of understanding each other, particularly in your new roles. It will work if you're both honest. There may be tears. ("I never dreamed you felt that way!") There may be laughter. ("That grates on your nerves? I can't believe it.") There should be healing and drawing closer.

You may want to go over this again each year, or every two or three years, to see if either of you have changed. If you're truly honest and open with each other and take the time to communicate, you will probably never have a need to do this again. Once you have been this honest, it will be easier to continue.

You will not only learn a lot about each other, you will learn a lot about yourselves. You will both know better what your needs are. The suggestions in parentheses are only springboard starters, to get you thinking.

• *I Need:*

(For you: more time for myself/my family/Mom; more money, a sense of peace.

For Mom: Better health; more communication with family; to see my grandchildren more often; to stop complaining and count my blessings.

For both of you: Is there one thing that would set your life aright, make your path smoother?)

• *My Greatest Strength Is:*

(For you: my love for my mother; my sense of humor; my ability to get along with others.

For Mom: patience, faith.)

• *My Greatest Weakness Is:*

(For you: an inability to delegate responsibility; a short temper.

For Mom: feeling sorry for myself; wallowing in my loneliness.)

• *The Best Advice I Ever Received:*

(For you: could be from a parent, spouse, the Bible. Why was it such good advice? How does it help with your caregiving?

For Mom: in what ways has it helped you in your ripening years?)

• *The Worst Advice I Ever Received:*

(Same as above.)

• *The Most Important Lesson I Have Learned:*

(For you: from your experience, as a young person, or in your recent past. What effect has it had on your life? On your caregiving? Your relationship with your mother?

For Mom: Did you learn it early or late in life?)

• *I Look Forward To:*

(For you: resigning from the rat race; having grandchildren.

For Mom: the rest of my life.)

• *I Dread:*

(For you: growing old; Mom dying; children leaving home. For Mom: the lonely times; failing health; running out of money.)

• *I Am Happiest When:*

(For you: I am with family; alone; with my husband; with Mom.

For Mom: I am connected to all members of my family; I feel well; I am free of pain.)

• *I Am Never Surprised When:*

(For you: life goes sour; everything turns out right; life is not fair.

For Mom: when young people ignore me; someone is nice to me.)

• *Everyone Should Learn To:*

(Handle money and time wisely; be kind; enjoy being alone; be optimistic.)

• *My Advice to Young People:*

(What is the one thing you wish all young people would do: strengthen their morals? love everyone? think well of themselves? Why?)

• *I Love:*

(Probably many things, such as beautiful music, a clear day, snow, flowers. What one person and/or thing do you love the most?)

• *I Can't Stand:*

(What grates on your nerves, makes you angry: cloudy days, insincere people, liars, gossip?)

• *I Wish:*

(If your fairy godmother appeared and granted you one wish, what would it be? Not world peace, get personal! Be careful what you wish for: You're going to get it!)

CHAPTER 24

Be Good to Yourself

You already know that most worthwhile things don't come easily, so you didn't expect your caregiving to be a snap. However, you don't have to be a martyr either. Your mother is going to live for quite a while, probably into your old age, and martyrdom won't hold up.

If your mother calls whenever she feels like it, or calls and complains about every little thing, real or imagined, or calls at inconvenient times, get an answering service. Then you can cope when you feel like coping. This may sound cruel. Poor, dear old lady! All alone and nothing to do and no one to talk to, and her caregiver gets an answering service.

The truth is, the dear old lady is being cruel to you, so you have to make it easier for yourself.

If your mother is a complainer, explain to her that negative thoughts actually affect her body and that with positive thinking she will be healthier. That goes for you too. You can tell her, if you want to, that that is one of the reasons you're getting an answering machine.

When you take charge, you eliminate a lot of resentment and hurt feelings. Mostly yours. When you're in control, you're calm. Realize that it's your own fault if you're running back and forth at your mother's whims. You are allowing yourself to become a victim, and it's up to you to stop it.

Daughters have complex feelings toward their mothers. She is the mother, and daughters often put unreasonable demands on themselves concerning her. It doesn't take a whole lot of time to become a full-blown martyr.

While you are being good to your mother—and to husband, children, employer, and so forth—don't forget yourself. You must have inner peace, and the only way you're going to have it is if you manage it. Tell yourself it's okay to rest, to take a vacation from caregiving, to do exactly what you want to do now and then. It is also perfectly permissible to say no.

Make schedules and stick to them. You don't have to be absolutely rigid, but you don't want to be blowin' in the wind either. For example, if you schedule Monday for grocery shopping and your mother says, "Oh, I've always shopped on Friday," smile and say, "Sorry, Mom. It has to be on Monday." Then drop the subject. It is not negotiable.

Even if, on every single Monday, your mother brings it to your attention that she would rather be shopping on Friday, don't let it get to you. Know that you are doing the best you can for your mother, for your family, and for yourself. If someone along the way doesn't like it, that's too bad, even if that someone is your mother.

If your mother calls on Wednesday and says, "I forgot to get mayonnaise. I had it on my list and then forgot to get it," and if she is in the habit of doing this, you say, "I'm sorry, Mom. Put it on your list for next Monday. I'll try to remember to remind you."

"But I need it now. I was planning on making potato

salad." Stick to your guns, even if it happens to be convenient for you to get a jar of mayonnaise and drop it off at your mother's. If you do, you will be setting a pattern that you won't want to stick to in the future. And don't worry about it. Did you ever hear of anyone dying because of lack of mayonnaise? If it is a matter of life or death, do anything you have to do. Once in a while you can accommodate your mother, of course, but for the most part stick to your schedule.

Since you're carrying an extra load, labor of love though it may be, it is still another load on your shoulders. As caregiver the wise thing to do is to schedule your time so that there is some time for you. Doing everything for everyone and having nothing for yourself does not make you a saint. It only shows how unorganized you are. If you set unrealistically high goals for yourself, you're going to burn out. I am being rough on you, but I want to spur you into being good to yourself so that you will last longer.

You can't tell your mother that you're trying to spread the work around so that you will still be there for her in ten or fifteen years. She is apt to sigh and tell you she doubts she will still be around in ten years. How do you argue with that? You simply have to do what you feel is right and you have to do it for yourself.

First of all, you can be more efficient at what you're doing. Read some of the books on the practical details of caregiving. (See Resources.)

If your mother's house is on fire or a raging flood threatens, you will have to deviate from your schedule. You might want to deviate from it now and then simply because you feel like doing something extra for your mother. Otherwise, no. You need time for yourself on a regular basis, for a nap, a walk, whatever relaxes you.

It would be a good idea to explain to friends and neighbors that you are a caregiver and that it's necessary for you to schedule your time. Ask them to call first rather than dropping in unannounced. Otherwise your frustrations will mount. For example, just as you settle down to a nap or a good book, there is a knock on the door. You say to yourself, "Well, if it isn't Mom making demands on me, it's someone else." So you don't enjoy your friend's visit and you might develop an ulcer. Plan ahead, not only for your free times, but for times with friends.

Remember that it's okay to say no. Even to your mother. She may try to make you feel guilty, but don't let her do it. Never say yes simply to avoid an argument. Even if tears well up in her eyes, look the other way. Say no graciously, with humor if possible, but do it.

Let your mother know that flattery won't work. If she says, "I am so lucky to have you," hug her and say, "I'm lucky to have you too." If she says, "You're so much kinder and nicer than your sister," hug her and say, "I know." Then continue to do exactly what you have already figured out you can handle.

If your mother gives you that disapproving look, ignore it. That look could once bring you to your knees, but you're a big girl now and you know what you're doing. If she greets you with cold silence, don't even ask why. She'll tell you. Listen, try to straighten it out, but don't be afraid of her.

Don't put up with a Nagging Nellie either. If your mother starts that, cut it off. "Mom, I have made my decision and I have told you my reasons. I'm not going to change my mind, so let's forget it."

When there are extracurricular events in your family, such as graduations, birthday parties, and so on, plan ahead.

Probably your mother can do for herself, maybe even help with the preparations. If not, hire someone to be with her for a day or two.

This is the only life you have, and you must go about it in the way that makes you happiest. This is not being selfish, it's being smart. You will make mistakes. No doubt your mother will warn you when she thinks you're making a mistake. Even if she's dead right and consequences have to be paid, it's your decision and you're the one who will pay. So do it your way.

Develop a positive attitude and don't let anyone, including your mother, destroy it. Anytime anyone presents a negative thought or idea, walk away. I have a friend who says, when anyone starts talking in a negative way, "I don't want to talk about that." It stops 'em cold.

I carry a small cloisonné whistle with me quite often. It reminds me to stay calm, and to wipe out unhappy negative thoughts. If I don't clear my mind, I am going to have to blow the whistle no matter where I am. It works for me. I have never blown the whistle. A stone from your driveway or a button will do as well. Keep reminding yourself, in some way, that you must be at peace. Nursing negative thoughts can make you ill.

There are many frustrations connected with caregiving. Some you can do something about, some you can't.

One caregiver's mother became incontinent. She bought pads to wear, but the daughter noticed that her mother smelled of urine. Her mother, with her decreased sense of smell, obviously was unaware of this. The daughter couldn't take on the extra burden of washing her mother's clothes, she hated to tell her mother that she smelled bad, but she couldn't simply ignore it. Talk about frustration! Eventually she was good to herself. In a loving way she talked to her mother about it. At first her mother cried. "Oh, how terrible it is to get old!" The daughter said, "Oh, it's not so terrible. Just rinse out your clothes every day and hang them in the bathroom to dry. Remember, it's not how you look or feel that really matters. It's how you smell that counts." The tension was relieved and the daughter's frustrations vanished.

Another caregiver was cleaning her mother's house and found a jar stuffed with money. When she asked her about it, her mother said, "Well, I certainly don't trust banks. They cheat people. I have always saved my money and hid it."

"You mean there is more?"

"Of course. I hid it all in jars."

When the daughter tried to get her mother to tell her where the rest of the money was, the mother said, "I won't tell you. That's my personal business."

This was certainly frustrating, but the daughter decided not to let it worry her. She asked her mother to write down the hiding places and to keep that slip of paper in a special, secret place. Her mother was willing to do that, and the daughter didn't have to have nightmares of one day having to tear her mother's house down in order to find the jars of money.

The first thing to do is to realize how many of these frustrations you can turn around. Then, with a positive, be-good-to-yourself attitude, resolve not to let the others drive you crazy. Draw on your faith for strength and peace of mind. ("I know how to be abased, and I know how to abound: everywhere and in all things I am instructed both to be full and to be hungry, both to abound and to suffer need. I can do all things through Christ which strengtheneth me." Philippians 4:12–13)

Pollyanna found something good in everything. We laugh now at the "Pollyanna attitude," but what do you want to bet she was emotionally healthy?

You want your relationship with your mother to be as good as possible. Caregiving isn't all a bed of roses for your mother either, you know. Remember the long-ago day when you cried, "I didn't ask to be born!"? Maybe your mother is saying, "I didn't ask to live this long!"

Call the positive things to your mother's attention. Instead of letting her complain about the heat and humidity, for example, talk to her about how comfortable it is with air-conditioning. Ask her what it was like in the summer before air-conditioning.

Refuse to be a victim. If you are, it's almost always because you allowed it. You have options, so make the right choices. There do not have to be any victims. Let's say that it's the end of a busy day and you're exhausted. You sit down, put your feet up, and sigh. You're looking forward to a quiet, restful evening with your family. The phone rings. Your mother says, "There's a package at the post office for me. I know it's that embroidery material I've been waiting for. The post office is open until five. Could you possibly go and get it for me?"

This is not a life-or-death situation. Your mother can wait until tomorrow for her embroidery material. Still, she sounded so excited, so happy that it had finally arrived. You know if you don't go and get it and take it to her, you're going to feel guilty as hell. So you sigh again, drag yourself out to the car, and go to the post office. You are a victim and it's your fault.

You could just as well respond to your mother's enthusiasm, assure her you will do what you can to get the material to her, and then sit down and figure out how you can do it without being a martyr. Can you call the school and ask one of your kids to take care of it on the way home? Or would it be convenient for your husband to do it? You could tell your mother that you're glad the material has finally arrived and say, "I can't go and get it tonight, Mom. I'll tell you what, I'll go to the post office first thing in the morning. You have a pot of coffee ready and we'll look at the stuff together."

Then you can go back to your easy chair and know that you are not a victim. You're in control. You haven't had to scream or yell or make anyone unhappy. You made the best of the situation, and there weren't any victims at all.

One woman wrote, "I was my mother's caregiver for eighteen years. She made me feel guilty every single day. There was always something I did or didn't do or could have done."

This can happen to you if you're not in control.

Let others do things for you. One mother was feeling blue because of something that had happened in the family. A neighbor told that mother's caregiving daughter, "I'm taking your mom out to lunch and a movie. She needs cheering up." Even though the daughter had planned something along those lines herself, she very wisely let the neighbor take her mother out.

When someone offers to do your mother's laundry or take her shopping, don't automatically say, "No, I always do that." Sure you do, but be good to yourself and learn to recognize serendipity. When a surprise bonus comes your way, grab it. Don't wait to be surprised, though. Make suggestions to your older children. "Grandma is due to have her eyes checked. She would love it if you would take her."

Some colleges offer an Adult Sitter Clinic for persons seeking employment as sitters with homebound elderly. Find out if there is such a course at your local college and get the names of people who have completed the training.

Some states have passed legislation providing for certain types of unpaid leave of absence without loss of health coverage or other employment benefits. Also, the laws help ensure job security on return to work. In April 1988 Wisconsin enacted a comprehensive family-leave law. This offers employees unpaid leave to care for a newborn, ill child, or elderly relative. About fifteen other states have passed family-leave laws.

And don't lose your enthusiasm: it is a marvelous trait that you can develop. Most of us, most of the time, don't give a hoot about much of anything. ("Shop at the new mall? Sure, why not?" "How did I like the movie? Okay, I guess.")

Look at children and how enthusiastic they are over the simplest of pleasures. Try to recapture that. Watch people who are enthusiastic: it's contagious.

If possible, change your routine. Many grocery stores are open at night and you and your mother could go out for dinner and shopping now and then. If your mother's home needs a little extra cleaning, get some of your friends to join you in the cleaning and your mother can furnish lunch for everyone. Later you can do the same for your friends. Don't always shop at the same store or eat at the same restaurant. Ask your mother for ideas. ("Is there something you would especially like to do? Somewhere you want to go?")

Try new things. Get in the habit of saying, "What if I ... ?" and "Maybe I could ..." You have at least a million brain cells you probably aren't using and creative thinking will put them to work and help to make life more interesting and pleasurable for you and your mother.

Now, the following may sound very whimsical, but why not indulge? It could be good for you. Adopt a muse to call upon when you're feeling negative and less than creative, or when you have a problem you're having a hard time solving. I adopted one years ago and I call on her all the time for help in my writing and creative processes.

You have a choice:

- Calliope—muse of beautifully voiced eloquence
- Clio—muse of history
- Euterpe—muse of music and lyric poetry
- Melpomene—muse of tragedy
- Terpsichore—muse of dance
- Erato—muse of erotic poetry
- Polyhymnia—muse of sacred poetry
- Urania—muse of astronomy
- Thalia—muse of comedy

These are from Greek mythology and aren't to be taken literally. Just pretend. My muse is Calliope, and sometimes, just before I go to bed, I say, "Okay, Calliope, you don't need to sleep, but I do. So work on this problem and get back to me in the morning."

Nearly always the answer is there for me in the morning. I know that it's really my very efficient computer brain at work, but it's fun to thank Calliope. If you don't like any of the muses from Greek mythology, make one up. She can be named Minnie Mouse or Tillie the Toiler, it's your muse.

There are some, I know, who will say, "How terrible! We are to call on the Lord for help." Well, I know that, and of course He is truly my rock and my fortress. But I say a little fun, a little fantasy, not as a substitute for the real thing, is fine.

Every now and then your caregiving duties, plus all the other things you do, may pile up and you'll find yourself angry. Or sad. Or drained. Go ahead and rave and rant and throw things. Cry your heart out. Go someplace where you can scream. Get it out of your system. Then, as soon as possible, return to your positive attitude. It's a way of being good to yourself.

Look into every area of your life and search for ways in which you can be good to yourself. Following are a few suggestions:

• One caregiver said, "Every Sunday we pick up Mom and go to church. Then back to our home for dinner. And Mom stays and stays. My husband retreats to the garage. Sundays have become very unpleasant."

Why not have a friend in the church pick up your mother and take her home every other Sunday? Or at least once a month. Whenever you can afford it, eat out. Take your mother home from the restaurant. This is necessary because otherwise your marriage could suffer. Your mother is important to you, but your husband comes first. He may simply want you to be there while he mows the lawn. He probably prefers not to have his mother-in-law there every weekend.

• *Consider hiring a helper.* Provide room and board in your mother's home in exchange for help. The helper can buy groceries, run errands, keep the house clean. If your mother lives near a college, a student might be very willing to do this.

• *Consider networking.* This is a valuable tool and it's not new. Years ago the farm community pitched in to do the threshing, to build a barn. Networking is a coming together of people and resources in order to make something happen. A group of caregivers that all have cars and all have elderly mothers can pool their resources and double up on trips to the store, doctor, and so on. Working as a team is networking. Check your phone book for local associations or call your Area Agency on Aging.

• *Take care of your physical self.* Pay attention to your diet and get enough exercise. Regular exercise is a great stress reducer. A brisk walk, or some form of aerobic exercise, relieves tension and gives you a sense of well-being. Get enough sleep. You will grow old more gracefully if you care for your body now. Initiate an overall program designed to keep you fit.

• *Do more new and different things.* Develop a hobby, go back to school. Instead of going to a restaurant, take a picnic and enjoy the outdoors. Leave the car at home and ride a bike to work. Don't get stuck in a rut, because the older you get, the deeper the rut gets.

• *Be careful about money.* Don't indulge your children, or you will regret it. If your almost-grown and grown children need money and you have it, don't give it to them. Loan them the money, with a signed agreement and a definite date by which the money is to be paid back. You'll be showing them what it's like in the world, and that's your job. At least one of your children will one day be your caregiver, and you want them to know the value of money. Teach them, by example, how to be sensible and prudent in the use of credit cards. You are on the path to your own old age, and if you haven't learned to be wise concerning money, you're going to be in trouble.

• *Plan very carefully for your own retirement.* As you care for your mother, take note of what works and what doesn't, what actions should have been taken long before. Don't neglect this. Encourage your husband to make plans too. Retirement knocks some people off their feet. Don't overplan, however. One woman said, "I was so afraid of retirement that I planned some activity for every day. I wore myself out! I forgot to plan on hours and days when I could do anything I pleased."

• *If your life is going wrong in some area, correct it.* This could involve a soured relationship, a long-held grudge, something you can't forgive. If you don't correct it now, it will lie in your heart, dormant. When you're old and have time to reflect, it will awaken, and become a huge regret that will sadden you and sour your old age.

• *Don't give up your friends.* Nurture them. You need dialogue and interaction with your peers. They will help keep you tuned in to the real world. One caregiver wrote, "My mother has become a huge pain in the neck. I have given up my social life in order to care for her and now that's all I have. Mother. And she expects one hundred percent of me."

Be good to yourself. You're worth it.

SECTION IV

The Final Days

*Cast me not off in the time
of my old age; forsake me
not when my strength faileth.*

—PSALM 71:9

CHAPTER 25

When You Can't Do
It Any Longer

You have been your mother's caregiver for a few years now. She is doing fine. You helped her through her grief and depression when Dad died, and between the two of you, you have settled into a routine that works. There have been no major crises, Mom's health is excellent, and it looks as though you're in this together for the long haul.

The only trouble is you're not as young as you once were. You still have the ongoing care of your children and husband, and you feel as though you're losing your identity. You have worked hard to get everything running smoothly and now you feel as though you're in a rut. Life simply isn't joyful anymore.

Maybe your mother has become too dependent on you. This could be your fault, of course, if you started out doing too much for her, but it's not too late to change. You can either let your mother know that there are certain things you can't keep on doing for her or you can get others to take over some of the tasks.

Perhaps because of your caregiving you feel that you can't continue working at a full-time job any longer. Still, you love your job and/or you need the money. You want to make the best decision and you don't need an added burden of guilt because of it.

You can handle it. Things have happened that turned your life around and you handled it, didn't you? What if your husband came home one day and announced, "I'm being transferred to the West Coast"? Your mother has lived in the same house on the East Coast for many years and will not move. You have no choice. You will go with your husband, keep in close touch with your mother, and maybe someday she will decide to move closer to you. Maybe she won't. You do what you have to do, what circumstances dictate you must do, and you don't have to feel guilty.

No one with an IQ over 50 should allow a joyless life to continue. But what do you do? Dump your mother? Tell her she's on her own and you hope she can make it for the next ten, maybe more, years? Or do you put your family on hold until your mother dies? Or do you stay in your tedious rut, feeling like an overextended zombie, watching the real you fade away?

You could do as one caregiver did: She stopped performing many of her caregiving acts of love. When her mother finally asked her what was wrong, she burst into tears and said, "Because there's never anything left over for me!"

It's too easy to make the elderly feel guilty for hanging around so long, and this response was a blow to the woman's mother. The family felt sorry for both of them but didn't know what to do about it. The caregiver was more unhappy than before, feeling guilty and mean and selfish.

There is a better way. Even though your caregiving has been fairly easy, it's not unusual for you to feel put upon and just plain weary. The body gets tired after all. When we push it too hard for too long, it protests and we suffer.

The reason you must do something about it is that this

caregiving will probably be required for quite a few more years. Also, you must remember that in all probability somewhere down the line the caregiving will become more involved and time-consuming.

Regardless of your attitude, the reality is that you are not as indispensable as you think you are. There are others who can perform many services for your mother and do them better than you can. Your first step to freedom will have to be to admit this.

More and more services for the elderly are popping up every day. Also, support groups for caregivers. Investigate. Find out how they can help you and pull you out of the rut. Talk it over with your mother. Believe it or not, she may be quite receptive. Seeing someone besides you, week in and week out, may be a most welcome change. Also, your mother has probably noticed how tired you are, and she will be happy to ease your burden.

You and your husband and family are entitled to a vacation once a year, and you must take it. Go to new surroundings and enjoy yourself. If you can't afford to take a trip, stay home. Announce that this is your vacation. For one or two weeks you will take walks, sleep late, go to dinner and the movies. You will not be available to anyone, including your mother.

When my kids were young and we had little money for vacations, I stayed home with them and we bowled, went to movies, and enjoyed each other. We also took what we called "flip trips." I would drive for five minutes, stop, and one of the kids would flip a coin. "Heads. Turn left." And so on until a designated time. Where we were at that time was where we spent an afternoon or the night. Vacations don't have to cost a fortune. Mini-vacations offer respite too.

You can figure out some way for your mother to receive

minimal care for two weeks. Early in the game it will probably be enough for her to have a designated person she can call in an emergency. She can take a taxi to do her shopping.

One caregiving couple didn't take a vacation for several years because the wife's mother was dying. Even though her mother was well cared for, it seemed cruel to take off on vacation when she was about to draw her last breath any day. The trouble is, it took her mother three years to die, and before she did, the caregiver's husband died.

Assistance is going to vary a lot, depending on the state and city in which you live. Listed below are some of the services offered around the country. If such a program isn't offered where you live, consider setting it up yourself. For example, in some cities a Dial-A-Ride program for the elderly is available. The older person calls a central number, explains her need (a visit to her doctor, the grocery store, etc.) and a volunteer is contacted to give her the ride. You could initiate this in your church, within your circle of friends, or maybe in your mother's neighborhood. I said initiate it, not do all the work.

You can go to your local Social Security office and ask what is offered in services for the elderly in your community. Or call the local Department of Social Services or Human Resources or the local Office on Aging. You can also find out what they will do to help you start a program. Or check with your pastor, or local newspaper, or the white and yellow pages of your phone book.

Some services you might want to look into include the following:

• *Local maid service.* These are teams who are trained to enter a home and do surface cleaning from one end to the other. They dust, sweep cobwebs from corners and ceilings, vacuum, clean bathrooms and kitchens, wash windowsills. The cost is surprisingly reasonable.

• *Visiting nurse services.* Go to a local hospital or ask your doctor. If your mother is laid up or ill for a few days or weeks, the added burden could be intolerable. Get names and phone numbers and find out how much this service costs. Then determine how it will be paid. Do all of this *before* a crisis occurs.

• *Homemaker and home health aides.* Check these out carefully. Insist on references; ask questions of former employers and teachers. Some are well-trained, responsible people; some are not. Licensing requirements exist for some, but not for all home-care workers. Some local universities have courses to train people to care for the elderly in their homes. On occasion this could be a lifesaver. Homemaker and home health aides are trained to handle household and personal care. Usually they will work under the direction of a professional. This may be a nurse or a social worker. They are not professionals and they are not maids, but they are trained to take care of the house and give necessary care to the elderly. (See Resources.)

• *Meals On Wheels.* If your mother goes along with this, it could be marvelous. There is no charge, but donations to keep the program going are welcome. A hot noon meal is delivered to the elderly person's home. Every recipient to whom I have talked said there is always enough food left over for a light supper. The volunteers who deliver the meals are friendly, loving people who are willing to stay for a few minutes' conversation every day. Your mother might love this service. It would certainly cut down on her grocery shopping and food preparation.

There is also a Federal Nutrition Program for the elderly. Nourishing, low-cost meals are provided to anyone sixty and over in churches, community centers, and schools. The purpose of this program is two-fold: to provide nourishing meals for the elderly and also to combat the isolation so many old people suffer.

• *Telephone Reassurance Program.* Volunteers call regularly at an agreed-upon time. If the elderly person doesn't answer the phone, the caregiver or a neighbor who has a key to the elderly person's home is notified. If this service isn't available in your town, try to get a friend or neighbor or another elderly person to make this call each day. It's a small thing, but it is one more responsibility that can be lifted from your shoulders. You won't have to think about it unless you get a phone call. You can call your mother whenever you feel like it, of course, but the point is you can do it when you feel like it and not calling won't add guilt.

• *Repair and maintenance services.* If your mother lives in an apartment, she already has this service, but if she is in a house, she's on her own. Screens need to be put up and taken down, lawns mowed, leaves raked, a fallen tree branch removed, a leaky faucet fixed, and bushes pruned. Of course, there are people who can be paid to do all of these tasks, but if your mother can't afford it, it falls to the caregiver to do it or have it done.

Quite a few churches maintain a list of members who are willing and able to do certain tasks for the elderly. All your mother has to do is call the church office, state her problem, and arrangements will be made for the appropriate volunteer to handle it for her. If your church doesn't have such a program, talk to the pastor about initiating one. That's what Christianity, and the Church, is all about: helping our brothers and sisters.

A word of caution: A woman wrote that her mother's neighbors always mowed her mother's lawn, picked up fallen branches in her yard, and made sure her driveway was clear and swept. This caregiver was grateful for the helpful neighbors but somehow never got around to thanking them or acknowledging their services. She found out later, when it was almost too late, that the neighbors resented having to do this. The reason they did the work was simply because they lived next door to the old woman and if her place was messy, it reflected on them. Just in time the caregiver and her husband treated the neighbors to dinner in a nice restaurant and the problem was resolved. "That taught me a lesson," this caregiver wrote. "Now when anyone does anything for my mother, I make sure they know how much it's appreciated." Don't assume that people help out of the goodness of their hearts and that that's their reward. They do, but they like to be thanked too.

• *Visitation programs.* Some communities and churches have volunteers who stop in at certain designated times for short, friendly visits. Perhaps the most important thing they do is listen. Most of the elderly lead a very solitary life, and providing someone to talk to, someone to listen even for twenty minutes or so now and then is a great service. You can stop feeling so sad (and so guilty) about your mother's isolation, and your mother can talk with someone besides you now and then.

Maybe you could arrange for some other elderly women to get together with your mother for coffee and cookies. Even if it's only once a month, it would be a most welcome diversion for your mother and her friends. A trusted high school student, or one of your own kids, could take care of the transportation. If your mother has no friends, maybe you know of a woman in the same situation. Tell your mother she can do a good deed by being friendly with this woman. Always try to kill two birds with one stone!

• *Senior day care centers.* These are proliferating and are often connected with a local church. Maybe your mother wouldn't care to go every day, but it would probably be good for her, and you, to get involved. You could take her there in the morning and pick her up in the evening on your way home from work. She will have a lot to talk about, and you can feel joy watching her eyes sparkle as she tells you about the things she did, the people she met.

What if your mother insists that she is perfectly content with her life as it is? She tells you she has no desire at all to join a group or get involved in some community activity. "Just leave me alone," she says, "I am living my life exactly the way I want to live it."

You think your mother's life is dreadful. She gets up in the morning, spends at least two hours reading the newspaper, working the crossword puzzle, sipping coffee. During the day she watches a couple of TV shows, sews, keeps her apartment neat, maybe takes a walk, naps, reads. You feel she would be happier if she got out and got involved in something with others.

You may be right, but not necessarily so. What was your mother's life like before retirement? If she worked at a full-time job, was active in school and church activities, or led a busy social life with your dad, it could very well be that a quiet life is exactly what pleases her now. She may have been waiting for this for a long time. If this is the case, leave her alone. In time she may want to get out more, get back in the mainstream, and if she does, she'll let you know. Or she will just go ahead and do it.

On the other hand, you should be aware of the fact that

loneliness can do peculiar things. When a person is alone, day after day, seeing no one, not having any conversations or interactions with others, they can succumb to the lonely life, draw into a shell, and try to fool themselves into thinking that this is what they want. So they actually avoid contact with people. It may be a subconscious feeling: If I can't have it, I don't want it, which helps to remove the pain. If you think your mother is withdrawing in this way, gently try to ease her out of it. Have your children visit her, you call her more often, ask her to do something for you. ("You know what a rotten seamstress I am, Mom. Will you shorten these hems for me?")

Don't plunge in saying, "She's not busy enough. She needs this or that and I'll take care of it for her." Find out how your mother really feels, what's going on in her head, and then act accordingly.

• *Alternate homes.* I have seen this solution work very well. Mom spends the winter months in California, half of them with Sis in southern California and half with Sonny in northern California. She lives in her own home during the summer. Any practical combination of this could work, depending on where everyone lives.

• *Travel.* Many older people love to travel and are able to do it for the first time in their lives. If your mother desires to see Africa, don't be afraid for her. Help her make the necessary arrangements and let her go. Planning the trip will be energizing for both of you. I know a dear eighty-five-year-old woman who travels all the time. She recently returned from Sweden and shared with us the sights and sounds of that country.

If your mother would like to visit relatives and friends and see new places but is fearful of flying, you can help her. If you have ever flown and had to change planes at an airport like Chicago's O'Hare, you can understand your mother's feelings and fears. The airlines are willing to help. Check with them and have your mother taken care of for the whole trip. I know of many elderly women who travel alone and they talk of being taken in a wheelchair (which they thought was fun) through busy airports, of never missing a connection, of friendly, efficient, and helpful service. More will be available in the future as our aging population swells.

Besides making your caregiving easier on yourself, and probably more enjoyable for your mother, there are other things you can do to make your caregiving go well.

One caregiver noticed a peculiar odor in her mother's home. Her mother said she couldn't imagine what it could be. Finally an investigation revealed little dishes of leftovers that had been pushed back in the refrigerator and forgotten. Lettuce and tomatoes in the crisper were rotten. The caregiver cleaned the mess and from then on checked her mother's refrigerator.

Another caregiver's mother had put a TV dinner in the oven and forgotten about it and it caused a fire. From then on her mother refused ever to use the oven and she was also afraid to fry food. Her caregiver bought her a small microwave oven, taught her how to use it, and now regularly brings casseroles to her.

What the caregiver doesn't need is additional tasks. However, in small ways, as time goes on, more and more will be added to the caregiver's list of duties. Eventually it can very well prove to be too much. Think about that little thin straw and what it did to the camel's back.

If, as early as possible, you begin to investigate what help is available and take advantage of some of your options, you won't end up being overburdened and wondering how it happened.

If your mother has Meals On Wheels twice a week, for variety for her and a respite for you, if something happens and she needs it more often, it will be a simple thing to make a phone call and have the meals delivered more often. That's much better than scurrying around looking for phone numbers and trying to make arrangements in a frantic hurry in the middle of a crisis.

If you have a network of volunteers and/or professional people in touch with you and your mother on a part-time basis, and familiar with your circumstances, it will be easier to enlist more help if and when it's needed.

Keep an eye on how it's going. Ask your mother from time to time if she is satisfied with the arrangements. It might be wise, once in a while, to drop in unexpectedly when someone is at your mother's home.

However you work it, for goodness' sake, don't keep on adding burden upon burden, thinking you have to do it all. You don't, and it is almost certainly a happier situation for both you and your mother if you allow others to help. In the business world the best kind of manager is the one who knows how to delegate. It's important for you to know how to do it too.

CHAPTER 26

Retirement

When I retired, after working full-time for over twenty years, I cheered. At last! I could stay home, do as I pleased when I pleased, and have a lot of time to spend writing. However, my cheers faded rather quickly. I wasn't at all prepared for this new life.

Every night I set my alarm for 6:00 A.M. just as I had done for years. When the alarm went off, I bounded out of bed and was in the kitchen before I started asking myself why I was up so early. A long day stretched ahead of me and I hoped I could fill it.

I wasn't prepared, either, for the guilt I felt about taking a nap in the middle of the afternoon or when I ate dinner at nine while watching TV.

My writing self dried up. During the twenty-plus years in which I had worked and raised children, I had managed to write nine or ten books plus many articles. I wrote at the kitchen table, in the evenings and on weekends. Now I was free to write for hours each day, but I couldn't get started.

What had happened? I had truly looked forward to retirement for a long time, but now that it was here, I wasn't at all happy. I crocheted afghans, I watched a lot of TV. I wrote letters telling of my discontent. I even thought about going back to work. It took me two years to straighten out, enjoy my retirement, and become productive again.

If your mother has worked outside the home and is now retired, she will be experiencing some distress. The best thing you can do is to be sympathetic. Don't take the attitude that some young people did with me: "Hey, I'll change places with you any day!" Oh, sure! They would love to have this sixty-nine-year-old body and nothing to do.

Unhappy retirees feel as though a large part of their identity is gone. In order to help your mother through this period, here are a few suggestions:

You and your mother could drive to different sections of town, park the car, and get out and walk. If your mother spent years dashing to work, to the bank and supermarket, leisurely walks around town could be interesting and pleasant. Get reacquainted with your town through visits to the zoo, museums, and so forth.

It's up to your mother, of course, but there are many activities in the community in which she can get involved. You and she can explore some of these.

Help her to handle her finances wisely. Can your children be encouraged to visit her now and then? There is nothing like the enjoyment of grandchildren to enhance the retirement years.

Most of all be patient. Help where and when you can, and know that the adjustment period won't last forever. While you're helping your mother, think about your own retirement.

One caregiver kept her husband's retirement date a secret. "We don't want my mother to know he's retired. If she finds out, she'll figure we have plenty of time on our hands and she'll become more demanding than ever." It isn't necessary or advisable to keep this a secret from your mother. (Secrets have a way of being discovered and can cause hurt feelings.) You and your husband should plan your retirement years, tell your mother about your plans, and then live your life the way you want to. Let your mother know that retirement opens up time for you and your husband. You will continue your caregiving as always, but your extra time is yours.

Start making your plans immediately. (See Resources.)

CHAPTER 27

Housing Options

Since so few elderly women live with their children, the chances are that your mother will live alone well into her aging years. However, the time may come, sooner or later, when your mother will require more caregiving than you can provide. This may happen when she's in her seventies, eighties, or when she's close to one hundred.

Since the passing of the law that forbids adult-only housing (a prejudicial and extremely unfair law in the opinion of many), retirement communities may flourish.

A retirement community may be a village of houses or a high-rise apartment complex. If extras, such as a golf course, swimming pool, and social director, are offered, they can be very expensive.

In some you buy the house you live in and pay maintenance fees. In others you rent but may have to pay maintenance fees also.

Some elderly prefer to live with their peers in a quiet atmosphere, and a retirement community is ideal for them. Others don't care for this and prefer to remain in their home or apartment.

Whatever it is that appeals to your mother, help her in

making a decision. Even though she says she would rather stay where she is, introduce her to the retirement communities so that she will be aware of all the options open to her. Go with her to as many of these communities as you can. All old people don't have the same requirements, so take your time. Your mother might be able to sign up for a short-term rental, then she won't be stuck if she's unhappy there. Don't rush into any decision. Take plenty of time to investigate, compare, and think about it.

Also, remember to consider the future. Will the retirement community still meet your mother's needs when she is in her eighties and nineties?

Remind her that if she moves too far away, she'll have less contact with you and your children except by phone.

Some factors to consider:

• Do the facilities suit your mother's life-style? (If she's very active, look for recreational and cultural activities.)

• What do some of the residents say about the community?

• Find out what insurance they have that will protect your mother in case they have financial problems.

• Find out about restrictions: Can your mother have overnight visitors? Can her grandchildren visit? Can her guests join her for meals in the dining room? How much will the meals cost?

• As with everything in this world, costs will go up, so in your planning, figure in these increases.

• When you decide on a community, be sure you receive written copies of all verbal promises, as well as the terms of the deposit.

• Mobile home communities: There are many of these, particularly in warm climates. Some have double mobile homes with dishwasher, washer and dryer, fireplace, and adequate space. These parks range from bare and unattractive to beautiful with trees and flowers. Costs vary accordingly.

• Homes for the aged: These homes are operated by private interests and by religious, professional, or labor organizations. These are homes where older people can maintain a good quality of life. There are social, recreational, and educational opportunities, and the residents are free to come and go as they wish.

CHAPTER 28

Nursing Homes

One woman wrote, "I had to put my mother into a nursing home. I was in such turmoil with guilt and with being torn two ways between my mother and my husband of forty-six years, neither of whom would let go. My pain was intense."

Only 6 percent of the elderly population ends up in nursing homes. Many more, after an accident or illness, go to convalescent hospitals, get well, and return home.

A nursing home, or convalescent hospital, isn't always a last-ditch, terrible alternative. If, for example, your mother has broken a hip or suffered an injury that will take a long recuperation, a convalescent hospital would be a godsend. Or if your mother hasn't been eating properly and is obviously suffering from malnutrition, a stay in the hospital could not only make her well again but could afford her the opportunity to learn more about good nutrition and help her to determine to eat more healthful foods.

Old people can be divided into two categories: those who can manage their own daily affairs and needs, with some assistance from others, and those who are totally dependent, including the senile. The latter probably belong in a nursing home.

Adult children are very reluctant to place parents in nursing homes. It is one of the hardest decisions they ever have to make. Many feel that to place their parent in a nursing home is to abandon them. Their feelings of shame and misery at the thought of assigning a stranger the responsibility of caring for their parent reflects the very strong antinursing-home sentiment that prevails in this country.

There may be any number of reasons why you must place your mother in a nursing home. One caregiver had to put her mother into a nursing home for several months because her mother was grieving over the death of a son. Her grief was so profound that she failed to eat, couldn't sleep, and was suffering from frequent fainting spells. After a few months in the nursing home, with round-the-clock care and attention, her mother was ready to go back home and resume her life. Whatever the reason, you will hate doing this, probably leave it until the very last minute, and guilt will plague you. You recall your mother saying, years ago, "Just don't ever put me into one of those nursing homes!" and you replied, "Oh, no, Mom! Never!" and here you are, knowing that's exactly what you have to do.

Your mother made similar painful, letting-go decisions when her children were young. She knows how much it can hurt.

You may have to place her in a home in order to save your marriage, your family life, yourself. If your mother has become impaired mentally or physically to the point where she can't take care of herself, you may have no choice. You haven't failed her.

You will have to consider the following: other family

members, power of attorney, the sale perhaps of your mother's home, her doctor's evaluation, her possible eligibility
for Medicaid, and other financial sources. If you and your
mother explored homes in advance and made the necessary
decisions some time ago ("Just in case, Mom") this will go
fairly smoothly for you. If you didn't, it will probably be
very difficult.

If at all possible, your mother should be included in this
decision and in the choosing of the nursing home. Your
mother's doctor will tell you the type of nursing home she
needs.

When you visit nursing homes, with your mother if
possible, the first thing to look for is their willingness to let
you explore. If you sense that they are hiding something or
are reluctant to answer your questions, go elsewhere. There
are good, efficiently run homes with nothing to hide. If your
mother receives Medicaid or Medicare, she may not have a
broad selection of nursing homes.

When you visit different nursing homes, look for the
following things (carry a notebook and pen and jot down
your reactions):

• A home close enough so that you can visit often.
• Uncrowded, lighted rooms that afford some privacy
and space for your mother's personal belongings.
• Facilities: Are there rails along hallways and in bathrooms? Is the lounge pleasant? Are the rooms clean and
odor-free?
• Condition and behavior of the residents: Are they out
of their beds, engaged in some activity, maybe reading or
watching TV? Are they clean or do they appear unkempt?
Don't be too upset by the actions and appearance of some
of the residents. People are in nursing homes because they

can't function on their own, so someone with a gaping mouth or staring eyes, or someone who is falling asleep in the middle of a checker game is not necessarily a reflection on the nursing home.

• Medical requirements: Will your mother have a complete physical examination by a resident doctor before entering the home? Is a doctor on twenty-four-hour call? Is the nursing and attendant staff large enough? Are tranquilizers used?

• Proximity of nearest hospital: If there is an emergency, to which hospital will your mother be taken and how will she be transported?

• Cost: How much does it cost and exactly what is included? Are there any extra charges? Will they help you obtain financial assistance if needed?

• A week's menu. Is the dining room attractive?

• A current state operating license.

• Access to parks, cinemas, libraries, and so on.

• Staff: Are they courteous and respectful? Supervised by a licensed nurse?

• Activity programs: Are they diverse and would they appeal to your mother?

Each state is required to have a nursing-home ombudsman, a representative who investigates claims and complaints. Contact your local or state office to get the name of the ombudsman. For further information on nursing homes, refer to Resources.

Once you have chosen the best possible nursing home, concentrate on your mother. Even though she may have agreed that this is the best solution, she will be frightened. Her way of life is being turned upside down. What little independence she has left will be taken from her. If possible, let your mother make every decision, down to the day she enters the home, and decide what she will take with her. She will be able to make a happier adjustment to her new life if she feels she has some control over what's happening. She needs to know that you aren't rejecting her.

Your mother's move to a nursing home may be directly from a hospital or from her home or yours. In any case, you want to make it as orderly and pleasant as possible. It is going to be traumatic for your mother, no matter how it's handled, and you will have a tough balancing act. You want to be efficient and at the same time loving and understanding.

If you can, let your mother make the decisions concerning when she will go, what she will take with her, and what is to be done with her possessions that she can't take.

Don't treat her like a child. False cheerfulness and remarks like "Isn't this a lovely place?" might work with a little child, but don't try to pull that on your mother. This is not a happy occasion, and your mother will be experiencing many sad feelings. So will you. Don't pretend they don't exist, but don't dwell on them either. Your mother is going to be angry. Maybe not particularly with you, but at the circumstances that led to this. She is going to have moments of depression and tearful silence.

You will be fighting your own feelings of sadness along with a sense of relief that will make you feel guilty.

One caregiver, forced to put her mother into a nursing home, kept up a running patter of how her mother was going to be better off. She didn't let her mother talk about her feelings, brushing it away with "Now, Mom, you know you're going to be happy." On the day her mother settled into her room in the nursing home, the daughter prepared to leave. "I'll be back to visit you often," she said.

Her mother replied, "Don't bother."

"Why not? Of course I'll visit you."

"No. Just leave me alone to die. That's why you brought me here, isn't it?"

Your mother will have a lot of possessions and she won't be able to take most of the them with her. Don't dispose of anything. Do your very best to see to it that your mother does that herself. It would be ideal if she could be home for a few days to do this. Even if she has to do it from a hospital bed, you take directions and follow through.

All of this will go more smoothly and with less sadness if you and your mother have discussed this possibility long before. If you have taken the time to say, "Just in case you ever have to go to a nursing home, what would you want me to do with this? and with that?" Your mother could even write it all down. Then, when the transfer to a nursing home becomes a reality, you can concentrate more on comforting your mother and letting her know how much you love her, easing the pain.

The more in control of this move your mother is, the better she will be able to adjust. Instead of "putting your mother into a nursing home," help her make a move that she knows is a necessary one.

Once in the nursing home, it's going to take your mother about six months to adjust to her new way of life. During this period keep in touch with her so that she doesn't feel that she's been deserted. Talk with the nursing-home staff and find out if they advise you to visit often. They may suggest that you stay away for a while so that your mother can settle in. You can write to her, send her cards and snap-shots. You can call. When it's right for you to visit her, don't neglect this. One of the saddest sights I have ever seen is a row of nursing-home residents on a Sunday afternoon. They were all dressed up, waiting for visitors that never showed up.

CHAPTER 29

The Final Crisis

Your mother will die. If death is swift and painless, or a matter of simply not waking up one morning, then you will plunge immediately into the aftermath of death. Getting through the funeral or memorial service and seeing to the distribution of your mother's belongings are done almost in a fog. You will have help, and if you have prepared yourself the best you can, you'll get through it.

However, what if your mother lies dying for hours, days, even weeks? The death of your mother is one of the most difficult things you have to face, regardless of how she dies.

You and your mother can prepare yourselves ahead of time to partly ease the pain. Her death is a certainty, and it doesn't make much sense to avoid the subject or act as if it won't happen. Talk about it. Be very honest in sharing your feelings.

"Oh, Mom, I don't know how I will be able to stand it!"

"Dear daughter, I know it will be hard for you, but it's the last thing I will ever do. Don't leave me to do it alone."

One woman wrote, "When my mother was dying, I

knew how she felt because we had talked about it many times. I knew that she was angry, so I didn't try to cheer her up. We were just angry together, and somehow it was comforting to both of us."

When the time comes and your mother is dying, remember your conversations about it. Treat it as the important and somber event it is. No false cheerfulness, no denying what is happening. Don't try to distract her by talking about everything but her dying. Don't act as though you don't believe this is happening. Acknowledge the fact that it most certainly is happening and that you and your mother have reached another milestone. Let her know that you will be with her to the end. Your mother is dying, but she is still your mother. She hasn't lost her mind, she is losing her life.

Don't allow anyone to visit her unless you and your mother have talked about it beforehand. Ask her to tell you who she wants near her during this time. It will probably be only her family. Above all don't let anyone come to her with a Bible and mini-sermons. If your mother has been a lifelong Christian, or even a short-term Christian, she doesn't need preaching. She has it all in her heart and is at peace with God. If she has not embraced a faith, it's a little late to try to scare her into some kind of foxhole conversion. Don't allow it. With your mother's permission a pastor might visit and bring comfort. She may have a friend with whom she can talk about faith and God and the assurances of Scripture.

Dying is a lonely act. No one can help or stop its progression. Let your mother have center stage. You stay in the wings and listen to her. Listen to her silence, if that's all there is. Hold her hand so that she can feel your touch and encourage her to say whatever is on her mind.

One woman said, "For years I refused to even think

about my mom dying. I knew the day would come, but I doubted that I would be able to handle it. It really scared me. However, after fifteen years of caregiving that grew progressively heavy for both of us, her death came as a kind of sweet release."

Let her go. Release her. The husband of a friend of mine was dying. He was suffering terrible pain. She and their son kept a vigil at his bedside praying, wiping his forehead, bringing him cool water. They prayed for healing, they told him it was going to get better. They held him and let him know how much they loved him.

Finally, after days of hoping and waiting, the son said, "Mama, we have to let him go." The son went to his father's bedside and said, "Daddy, Mama and I release you. We love you and we release you to God." Within hours the man was dead.

Even after death we have to release our loved ones. We do it with our minds and hearts, but it's almost physical. We must release the dying so that they can die in peace, and we must release our dead so that we can go on living in peace. This release is a conscious form of acceptance.

You and your mother can find comfort and some pleasure during these final days. You can look back on your life together. You can tell her what being her daughter has meant to you, and your mother can let you know how proud she is of you, how much she loves and appreciates you. This is a time to reflect on the continuity of the life cycle. Your mother may talk about her mother and then you and eventually the grandchildren she is also bidding farewell. Talk about the grandchildren and your hopes and dreams for them, how they will never forget their beloved Nana.

Remember, your mother has lived with the presence of death for a long time. She has known that each year brought her closer to it and she has, in her own private ways, prepared herself. If you two have talked about it and prepared together, these last hours will be more peaceful for both of you.

I know of one woman who knew she was dying and refused to see anyone. "I want to do this alone," she said, and she did. The dying person's wishes must be respected.

We have been looking at a picture of a peaceful death with your mother in her bed and you beside her, holding her hand. If you're lucky, that's the way her life will end. However, it may be far different. If your mother has cancer, or kidney failure, or any number of diseases, she will suffer, costs will be staggering, and you will go through hell.

There are some who say that in such cases the elderly should opt for a quick death, since our country can't afford prolonged, high-quality medical care for both its young and its old. If it were me and a young person nearby and we were both in need of a kidney and there was only one kidney, I would back out of the picture. Most old people would make the same decision.

However, there is a great danger here. Sometimes people feel that they have the right to decide whether or not their parent should be allowed to die. Or a doctor thinks he or she has the right to prolong life, no matter how senseless that life has become. People can be told about the possibilities and alternatives, but it is the dying person's decision. Maybe an old person will be willing to make that final sacrifice, whereas another will not, and that's okay; it must be their choice.

Another problem arises: Few are allowed swift and merciful deaths. We keep people going with machines. People with no hope of recovery are kept alive for no reason that makes any sense. They lie in hospital beds with tubes drip-

ping fluid into their bodies and medication keeping them
from hurting, which also keeps them from thinking. The
body is there, but the spirit is not. There can be no communication, no exchange of last words, nothing meaningful
until at last an exhausted soul slips away.

The caregivers of today comprise a generation that
promises to be the longest-lived in our history. The same
medical technology that is accomplishing this will be the
one that may keep you alive on a machine, with tubes drain-
ing into you, long after you have given up your life.

As your mother's caregiver, talk about all of this and
find out how she feels. How you feel isn't that important.
It's your mother's life and her death. It's important to face
all possibilities beforehand so that you can handle it cor-
rectly, with the least amount of pain and the way you know
your mother wants you to handle it.

Perhaps your mother will say, "Oh, I don't care. I only
hope I die quickly, that's all." In that case the deathbed
decisions will be yours. When my mother suffered a stroke,
I called an ambulance and rode with her to the hospital. As
we entered the lobby, a wheelchair was brought to her and,
in an amazing spurt of energy, she kicked the wheelchair
and sent it hurtling across the room. She was unable to talk,
but she looked into my eyes and I knew what she was thinking. We had discussed it many times. "I don't want to spend
my last hours in a hospital bed," she had told me, "connected to tubes, being waited on by strangers." So now,
with the wheelchair clattering against a wall, I asked if my
mother and I could have some time alone. We were put into
a tiny cubicle with a narrow bed and a chair, and I was able
to hold her in my arms while she died.

The doctor told me later that he could have rushed her
upstairs and taken emergency measures. "But the best you

could have hoped for would be maybe fifteen or twenty years of caring for a mother who would lie helpless in bed." I know how much my mom would have hated that.

Lately I have known several older people who, when told by a doctor that they have inoperable cancer, have simply refused treatment of any kind. Near the end they were given medication to relieve the pain. It seems that patients can accept the fact of death much better than the physicians can.

You can get, free of charge, the correct Living Will for your state. Write to the Society for the Right to Die, 250 West 57th Street, Room 323, New York, New York 10107. When your mother receives this form, make sure she signs it, has her signature witnessed by two nonrelatives, and puts it with her other important papers. Most states have a Living Will statute (you can find out if yours does by calling your local Area Agency on Aging). Even if your state does not have this statute, write a Living Will anyway, because often the courts will uphold it.

A Living Will simply states that you do not want to be kept alive by any artificial means. It would be a good idea for all members of the family, plus your mother's pastor or rabbi or priest and doctor to get together and discuss this. Your mother can make her wishes known. Then, in case it becomes impossible for her to communicate, you will have more than just yourself saying, "But I know this is what my mother wants."

There have been a few times, down times to be sure, when I have thought that I didn't care when I died. In fact it would probably to best to get it over with. I was just going from day to day, accomplishing little, contributing even less. Some said to me, "Oh, I envy you. You write books. You have a legacy to leave your children." That didn't lift my spirits. My children don't read my books, and I read somewhere that the shelf life of the average book is something like one week.

I normally have an upbeat, optimistic outlook. When my children talk about how tough life is, I am always there with the assurance that everything will work for the good. Life is great, I tell them, and God is good and nothing is ever as bad as it seems. I mean it too. However, as I grew older I began to experience down times. My children would have to face my death one day, I reasoned, and they could handle it as well now as later. I had the terrible feeling that I was taking up space for too long and for no purpose. When I had these feelings, they were accompanied by a sense of resignation. "Oh, well, what difference would it make?" This was so far from my usual self, it was frightening. So I called Heide and said, "Guess what crazy thing your mama has been doing? Thinking she might as well die now as later."

Heide responded by laughing. "Oh, great! Now I have to worry about you going off your rocker, huh?"

We talked about it and I described my feelings, and in the end we were able to agree that I had momentarily lost a few marbles.

If you are hesitant about bringing up the subject of death with your mother, don't be. Believe me, she has thought about it and perhaps, like me, in negative ways. Talking it over with you, making plans, should eliminate those lonely, negative times.

You can remind your mother of all the things there are yet to accomplish, of the sweet hours together you and she can still share. Let her know how much you love her so that she can get back her zest for life.

Now is the time when you need to talk to your husband

and close friends. Let them see and feel your sadness and give them the opportunity to console you. Lucy told me that she will remember forever what her friend did for her. Lucy's mother was dying and she sat at her hospital bedside around the clock. Lucy's friend came to her one afternoon and told her to go home and take a shower and a nap, and that she would sit with her mother until Lucy returned.

If you and your mother have had some running arguments, resolve them. If you don't, they will grow in importance and haunt you with guilt and remorse long after your mother's death.

As your mother dies, you won't be able to avoid thinking about your own death. None of us lives forever, and strange as this may seem, your mother's death may be your first encounter with this reality. If you can understand the truth about your own mortality, it should help you with living. It may help you to focus on the truly important things in life.

CHAPTER 30

Planning Your
Mother's Funeral

Funerals are not a pleasant topic. We don't like to talk about them, we avoid discussions about them, even though we know we should plan them.

Most of all we hate talking about how much the funeral will cost. We flippantly say, "Nothing is too good for my mother" and "I don't care what it costs, I want the best."

Spending a lot of money on your mother's funeral is not being good to your mother, and you know it. Believe me, you will care about the costs. And it will be much more difficult to be sensible if you leave the planning to a time when you're overwhelmed with grief, in a state of shock, and vulnerable to smooth sales pitches. Besides, why shouldn't your mother have a say in the planning? That means you have to take care of this before she dies.

When my mother died, a funeral director showed me some beautiful, very expensive chiffon dresses. "Don't you want to buy a nice dress for your mother?" he asked. (He knew that I was a widow with four young children. If I had known then what I know now, I would have gone to another funeral director!) "I never bought a dress like that for her when she was alive," I replied, "I don't see any reason to do it now."

I was able to be practical because my mother and I had talked about this before she died. I remembered her saying, "If you want to do something nice for me, I'd love to have a little portable TV. I'd enjoy that a lot more than wearing a beautiful dress in an expensive casket." She got the TV.

Do good things for your mother now while she's alive and can enjoy and appreciate them. Later you will feel much better about having been good to your mother. Giving her the best and most costly after she is dead means nothing.

Burying her in expensive trappings won't do much for your conscience or peace of mind. If you're wealthy, it still might give you more pleasure and satisfaction to give to a memorial or charity in your mother's name. Donate money to your church. If your mother loved books, give to the church or public library. My mother particularly admired the Salvation Army for their work, and a donation to them was made in her name. There are children's homes, shelters for battered women and the homeless.

The most expensive purchases most of us make are a home and a car. Did you know that a funeral can be the next most expensive outlay? The average funeral costs around $4,000 not including a cemetery plot, which runs around $300 to $400. (Call a funeral director and ask about costs. Federal law says they must give you price information, even over the phone. If they won't, go to another funeral director.)

Don't let a funeral director tell you that the body must

be embalmed, either. This is not always true and is certainly unnecessary if a person is buried within twenty-four hours or if the body is cremated. Some will try to tell you that embalming preserves the body. Why would you want to do that? Embalming costs between $150 and $250. Why spend the money if you don't have to?

My beloved father-in-law planned his own funeral years before he died. Along with choosing the sermon topic, the hymns, and other details, he also saw to it that the money to pay for it was available.

Some people write their own epitaphs. Ask your mother if she wants to do this. Find out if she wants to be buried next to Dad. Does she want to donate any organs? She may not have thought of these things, and they are her decisions to make.

My greatest concern is my children. I don't want any added pressures or inconveniences or expenses added to their grief. I have opted for cremation (with their approval) and chosen a prepaid plan that will be unaffected by inflation or any other reasons.

There are ways to make sure the money is available to pay for the funeral. Your mother and her principal caregiver can be cosigners on a savings account. At the time of the funeral it will be easy for the caregiver to withdraw the money and pay the funeral costs. Perhaps your siblings can contribute to a special account, a little each month or each year, until there is enough to cover the cost of a funeral. It's best to plan ahead and get the cooperation of others in advance. I have heard many horror stories of caregivers being forced to foot the entire bill. Too often, after the funeral, siblings and their wallets disappear. One caregiver asked each of her three siblings to pay one-fourth of their mother's funeral costs. She received excuses, tales of woe, promises, but no money. Months later these same siblings criticized her because she hadn't bought an elaborate headstone.

If your mother says, "I don't care what you do. I will be dead, so it won't matter to me," go ahead with your siblings and plan the whole thing. Be sensible regarding costs. When you all agree on a plan, show it to your mother. "This is what we plan to do. Is it all right with you, Mom?"

You may say, "We'll have an open casket at the funeral service so that everyone can say good-bye to you. Pastor Jones will preach a sermon and John will give a eulogy. We'll have one hymn, 'All Glory Laud and Honor,' and then we'll have a brief ceremony at the cemetery."

Even though your mother said that she didn't care what you planned, she may very well say, "Oh, no, that's not all right with me at all! The casket should be closed. I don't want people saying good-bye to me when I can't respond. I don't want a eulogy. And the hymn I love best is 'My Jesus, I Love Thee.'"

On the other hand, if her other children won't talk about the funeral, you should help with the plans, including details of how it will be paid, and once you and your mother agree, present the plan to the other children in writing.

For specific help in planning a funeral, turn to Resources.

When I was a child, funerals were large, social, family gatherings. It was a time when we got to see all the aunts and uncles and cousins, and there was a lot of food. People didn't live long lives in those days, so there were plenty of relatives to attend funerals. Today it's not unusual for a person to have outlived nearly all his or her relatives. One elderly lady said, "There won't be very many at my funeral. Everyone's gone on ahead of me. In fact I don't think I'll go either. Someone will just have to take me."

Ten Commandments
For A Caregiver

1. Honor your mother. Love her with all your heart. She is the only one you will ever have.

2. Don't let your mother run your life. Be loving, be gentle, but be in charge.

3. Don't be afraid of your mother. You're all grown up.

4. Be good to yourself so that you don't burn out.

5. Do not consider yourself mother to your mother. You are not and cannot be.

6. Don't patronize your mother or baby her. She has lost her youth, not her mind.

7. Do as little as possible for your mother for as long as possible. She needs to do for herself.

8. Plan your mother's last years with her, not for her.

9. Do not a martyr be.

10. Accept your mother's aging and her death. You have no choice, and acceptance brings peace and understanding.

RESOURCES

AGING

The Aging Game, by Barbara Gallatin Anderson. New York: McGraw-Hill Inc.

Alone—Not Lonely: Independent Living for Women Over Fifty, by Jane Seskin. Mt. Prospect, Il.: AARP Books/ Scott, Foresman & Co., 1985.

And God Created Wrinkles, by E. Jane Mall. New York: Ballantine/Epiphany Books, 1988.

The Better Half of Life, by Jim Geddes. Nashville, Tenn.: Broadman Press.

Growing Old—Feeling Young, by John W. Darkeford. New York: Ballantine/Epiphany Books, 1985.

Growing Old in America, by David Hackett Fischer. New York: Oxford University Press, 1977.

Growing Old, Staying Young, by C. Hallowell. New York: William Morrow & Co. Inc., 1985.

How a Woman Ages, by Robin Henig. New York: Ballantine Books Inc., 1985.

Learn to Grow Old, by Paul Tournier. New York: Harper & Row, Publishing, 1983.

Older People Have Choices, by Nancy Manser. Minneapolis: Augsburg Publishing House, 1984.

The Senior Adult Years, by Carroll B. Freeman. Nashville, Tenn.: Broadman Press.

Successful Aging, by Anne C. Averyt. New York: Ballantine Books Inc., 1987.

The View in Winter: Reflections on Old Age, by Ronald Blythe. New York: Harcourt Brace Jovanovich, Inc., 1979.

Why Survive? Being Old in America, by Robert Butler, M.D. New York: Harper & Row, Publishing, 1975.

ALZHEIMER'S DISEASE

Alzheimer's Disease and Related Diseases Association (ARDA), Suite 600, 70 East Lake Street, Chicago, Illinois 60601. Write for information on local support groups.

Alzheimer's Family Support Groups. U.S.F. Suncoast Gerontology Center, University of South Florida, Box 50, 12901 North 30th Street, Tampa, Florida 33612. Write for *Manual for Group Facilitators*.

Coping and Caring: A Guide for Families with Alzheimer's Patients, No. D12441. AARP Fulfillment Section, Box 2400, Long Beach, California 90801.

Help Begins at Home. Free booklet contains information on how to care for people confused and disoriented by the effects of Alzheimer's disease or senile dementia. Includes a series of dos and don'ts, plus a description of the International Center for the Disabled (ICD) concept of a Reality Orientation Room—a room in the home that contains a clock, easily read appointment calendar, chalk or bulletin board, plus a place for keys, hearing aids, and other frequently used items. For a copy of the booklet, send a stamped self-addressed number-ten-size envelope to ICD, Box BB, 340 East 24th Street, New York, New York 10010.

CAREGIVING

Caregiving. Des Plaines, Ill.: AARP Books/Scott, Foresman & Company.

Caregiving: Helping an Aging Loved One, by Jo Horne. Mt. Prospect, Ill.: AARP Books/Scott, Foresman & Company, 1985.

Caregiving—When Someone You Love Grows Old, by John Gillies. Wheaton, Illinois: Harold Shaw Publishers, 1988.

Caring Children of Aging Parents, by Ethel Burdell, 4835 East Anaheim Street, #210, Long Beach, California 90804.

Caring for Your Parents: A Sourcebook and Solutions for Both Generations by Helene Maclean. New York: Doubleday & Co., Inc.

Children of Aging Parents, 2761 Trenton Road, Levittown, Pennsylvania 19056.

Don't Give Up on an Aging Parent, by Lawrence Galton. New York: Crown Publishers, Inc., 1975.

Helping Your Aging Parents, by James Halpern, Ph.D. New York: Fawcett/Crest, 1987.

How to Help Older People, by Julietta K. Arthur. Philadelphia: J.B. Lippincott Co., 1954.

Miles Away and Still Caring: A Guide for Long-Distance Caregivers, No. D12748, AARP Fulfillment Section, Box 2400, Long Beach, California 90801.

NEWSLETTERS. Universities offer caregivers ongoing support

through newsletters. For information, write Gerontology Center, University of Kansas, 316 Strong Hall, Lawrence, Kansas 66045.

TELEPHONE ACCESS SYSTEM. The Illinois Department on Aging, along with the National Association of State Units On Aging, have set up a toll-free telephone access system to inform those caring for older people throughout the nation about meal and transportation programs, housekeeping assistance, and adult day-care programs. Call 800-252-8966 and the staff at Elderlink will provide the contact for the appropriate agency to assist a relative in another state.

The Thirty-Six-Hour Day, by Nancy L. Mace and Peter L. Rabins. Baltimore: Johns Hopkins University Press, 1982.

You and Your Aging Parent, by Barbara Silverman and Helen Hyman. New York: Pantheon Books, Inc., 1982.

Your Aging Parent, by John Deedy. Chicago: The Thomas More Association, 1984.

DEAF AND HARD-OF-HEARING

Better Hearing Institute, P.O. Box 1840, Washington, D.C. 20013 (800-EAR-WELL).

Center for Intergenerational Learning, Institute on Aging, Temple University, 1601 North Broad Street, Philadelphia, Pennsylvania 19122. (215-787-6970). Develops model programs, is a resource center and clearinghouse for information concerning intergenerational programs, and provides technical assistance and training.

National Association of the Deaf, 814 Thayer Avenue, Silver Spring, Maryland 20910 (301-587-1788).

Organization for the Hard-of-Hearing. Write or call for literature and enclose a long, self-addressed, stamped envelope: SHHH, 7800 Wisconsin Avenue, Department 6, Bethesda, Maryland 20814 (301-657-2248).

DEATH AND FUNERALS

Cemetery Goods and Services: Planning for Difficult Times, No. D13162. Discusses traditional and nontraditional burials, cremations, liners and vaults, sales tactics, veterans' benefits, and so on, plus a listing of helpful publications and information on how to find your nearest nonprofit memorial society. Write: AARP Fulfillment, 1909 K Street, N.W., Washington, D.C. 20049.

Concern for Dying, Room 831, 250 West 57th Street, New York, New York 10107 (212-246-6962). Write or call to obtain samples of the Living Will and also information on durable power of attorney.

Conference of Funeral Service Examining Boards, P.O. Box 497, Washington, Indiana 47501.

Consumer Guide to the FTC Funeral Rule: Information Funeral Directors Must Disclose. Write: FTC Public Reference Branch, 6th Street and Pennsylvania Avenue, N.W., Room 130, Washington, D.C. 20580. Represents the funeral licensing boards of forty-seven states and has information on funeral laws in those states.

DONOR CARDS:

American Medical Association, 535 North Dearborn Street, Chicago, Illinois 60610. Attention: Order Dept.

Deafness Research Foundation, 366 Madison Avenue, New York, New York 10017.

Eye Bank Association of America, 3195 Maplewood Avenue, Winston-Salem, North Carolina 27103.

National Kidney Foundation, 116 East 27th Street, New York, New York 10016.

The Living Bank, P.O. Box 6725, Houston, Texas 77005. Coordinates disposition of anatomical gifts and organ donations. Free donor card.

It's Your Choice: A Practical Guide to Planning a Funeral. AARP Books/Scott, Foresman & Company, 1865 Miner Street, Des Plaines, Illinois 60016. $4.95 (AARP members, $3.00); add $1.75 per total order for shipping and handling.

Living Through Personal Crisis, by Ann Kaiser Sterns. New York: Ballantine Books, Inc., 1984.

On Death and Dying, by Elisabeth Kübler-Ross. New York: Macmillan Publishing Co., 1969.

Prepaying Your Funeral: Some Questions to Ask. Free brochure. Send a postcard requesting Stock No. PF3862 (287) to AARP Fulfillment, 1909 K Street, N.W., Washington, D.C. 20049.

Society for the Right to Die, 250 West 57th Street, New York, New York 10107 (212-246-6973).

Tips on Planning a Funeral. Send $1.00 and a stamped self-addressed envelope to the Council of Better Business Bureaus, Department 023 Washington, D.C. 20042-0023.

EMPLOYMENT

Encore, Kelly Services, offers temporary jobs to the elderly. They can have work experience, earn money, and learn new skills. Check with local Kelly Services.

McDonald's. Hiring part-time workers over sixty-five. Check at your local McDonald's or write: McDonald's Corporation, McDonald's Plaza, Oak Brook, Illinois 60521.

FINANCE

Do-it-yourself Kit for Planning Your Will. Write: Hanley's, 22502 Orchard Lake Road, Farmington, Michigan 48024.

The Essential Guide to Wills, Estates, Trusts, and Death Taxes. AARP Books/Scott, Foresman and Company, 1865 Miner Street, Des Plaines, Illinois 60016. $12.95 (AARP members $9.45); add $1.75 per total order for shipping and handling.

Institute of Certified Financial Planners (ICFP), 9725 East Hamden Avenue, Denver, Colorado 80231. Will send you a free pamphlet of guidelines for choosing a financial planner.

International Association of Financial Planners, Suite 120C, 5775 Peachtree Dunwoody Road, N.E., Atlanta, Georgia 30342. Look in your phone book for a local chapter.

More Money for Your Retirement, by John Barnes. New York: Harper & Row, Publishing, Inc., 1978.

The Retirement Money Book, by Fred Nuaheim. Washington, D.C.: Acropolis Books, Ltd., 1982.

A Survival Kit for Wives: How to Avoid Financial Chaos Before Tragedy Strikes, by Don and Renee Martin. New York: Villard Books, 1986.

Sylvia Porter's New Money Book for the 1980s, by Sylvia Porter. New York: Avon Books, 1980.

HEALTH AND NUTRITION

Activity, Health and Fitness in Old Age, by Jean Macheath. New York: St. Martin's Press, Inc., 1984.

After Middle Age: A Physician's Guide to Growing Old and Staying Healthy, by Richard Jed Wyatt, M.D. New York: McGraw-Hill, Inc., 1985.

Booklet published by AARP tells you how to choose a doctor, good health habits, guidelines for social and emotional well-being, weight control and diet, and other ideas for staying healthy. Write AARP, Health Advocacy Series Program Department, 1909 K Street, N.W., Washington, D.C. 20049.

Jane Brody's Nutrition Book, by Jane Brody. New York: Bantam Books, Inc., 1982.

Columbia University Complete Guide to Health and Well-being After Fifty, by Robert J. Weiss, M.D. and Genell Subak-Sharpe. New York: Times Books, 1988.

Dietary Guidelines for Americans. Free brochure. Send a postcard request to the Food and Drug Administration, Office of Consumer Affairs, HFE-88, 5600 Fishers Lane, Rockville, Maryland 20857.

Diet for a Small Planet, by Frances Moore Lappé. New York: Ballantine Books, Inc., 1982.

Eating for Your Good Health, No. D12164, AARP Fulfillment Section, Box 2400, Long Beach, California 90801.

Health and Aging, by T. Hickey. Monterey, California: Brooks/Cole Publishing Co., 1980.

Mealtime Manual. Contains many good ideas for adapting homes for independent living, as well as recipes. Write: Campbell Soup Company, Box 38, Ronks, Pennsylvania 17572.

Medical Handbook for Senior Citizens and Their Families, by Dr. Howard Thornton. Auburn Publishing Co.

Nutrition Against Disease, by Roger J. Williams. New York: Bantam Books, Inc.

United Seniors Health Cooperative, Suite 500, 1334 G Street, N.W., Washington, D.C. 20005 (202-393-6222). Write or call for their easy-to-read *Guide to the Medicare Maze and Medical Bill Organizer*. Includes expandable file with nine dividers. $19.95 for the complete set.

HOME CARE

The Block Nurse Program. This is a community program that draws on the professional and volunteer services of local residents to provide nursing and other services to their elderly neighbors who might otherwise have to be admitted to nursing homes. For information contact: The Executive Director, The Block Nurse Program, 65 Langford Park, Saint Paul, Minnesota 55108 (612-644-4524).

Foundation for Hospice and Homecare, 519 C Street, N.E., Washington, D.C. 20002 (202-547-6568). For credited/approved agencies prepared by the National Homecaring Council (nonprofit) and for their publications.

Handbook About Care in the Home, No. D955. AARP Fulfillment Section, Box 2400, Long Beach, California 90801.

Help Through Respite Care Program. If you must leave an older person alone for a time, this program offers you a respite. You can take a break for days, weeks, months. This is offered through local hospitals, community groups, and public and private agencies. While you are away, everything that needs to be done will be done. For information call your state Office of the Aging.

Home Health Services and Staffing Association (Proprietary), 2101 L Street, N.W., Suite 800, Washington, D.C. 20037 (202-775-4707). Information on local agencies.

National Association for Home Care, 519 C Street, N.E., Stanton Park, Washington, D.C. 20002; (202-547-7424). Write for *All About Home Care: A Consumer's Guide* ($2.00) and *How to Select a Home Care Agency* (free).

Senior Companion Program. Volunteer help in your home. For information write: Senior Companion Program, 806 Connecticut Avenue, N.W., Washington, D.C. 20525 Or: National Association of Senior Companions, P.O. Box 1510, Opelousas, Louisiana 70570.

HOUSING

American Association of Homes for the Aging, 1129 20th Street, Washington, D.C. 20036 (202-296-5960). Free publications.

A Home Away from Home. Booklet. Information about board and care homes, choosing a home. AARP Consumer Affairs Department, 1909 K Street, N.W., Washington, D.C. 20049.

Housing Options for Older Americans, No. D12063, AARP Fulfillment Section, Box 2400, Long Beach, California 90801.

National Institute of Senior Housing, National Council

on the Aging, West Wing 100, 600 Maryland Avenue, Washington, D.C. 20024 (202-479-1200).

National Shared Housing Resource Center, 6344 Greene Street, Philadelphia, Pennsylvania 19144 (215-848-1220). Publishes a directory.

The Older American's Guide to Housing and Living Arrangements, by Margaret Gold. Mount Vernon, N.Y.: Consumer Reports Books.

A Place to Live in Your Later Years, by Paul B. Maves. Minneapolis: Augsburg Publishing House.

Where Can Mom Live: A Family Guide to Living Arrangements for Elderly Parents, by Dr. Vivian F. Carlin and Ruth Mansberg. Lexington, Mass.: Lexington Books.

Your Home Your Choice. A Workbook for Older People and Their Families. AARP Consumer Affairs Department, 1909 K Street, N.W., Washington, D.C. 20049.

INSURANCE

Catastrophic Coverage Under Medicare, No. D13299. AARP Fulfillment Section, Box 2400, Long Beach, California 90801.

Information on Medicare and Health Insurance for Older People, No. C38, AARP Fulfillment Section, Box 2400, Long Beach, California 90801.

LEGAL

American Bar Association—Commission on Legal Problems of the Elderly, 1800 M Street, N.W., Washington, D.C.

20036. Provides referrals to competent attorneys. Write for free booklet, *Doing Well by Doing Good*.

Legal Counsel for the Elderly. 1909 K Street, N.W., Washington, D.C. 20049. Offers self-help legal information.

LOVE AND SEX

Love and Sex After Sixty, by Robert N. Butler and Myrna I. Lewis. New York: Harper & Row, Publishing, Inc., 1977.

Love, Sex, and Aging, by Edward M. Brecker with the editors of Consumer Reports Books, Bridgeport, Connecticut, 1984.

MAGAZINES

Age Pages. Distributed free by the National Institute NIA Information Center, 2209 Distribution Circle, Silver Spring, Maryland 20910 (301-495-3455).

Lady's Circle. (Contains a "Golden Years" section.) Mailing Department, 105 East Thirty-fifth Street, New York, New York 10016. One-year subscription, $7.97. Also sold in supermarkets.

Mature Outlook. Write: Mature Outlook Organization, 3701 West Lake Street, Glenview, Illinois 60025-8205. Members, $3.00 per year; others, $6.00 per year.

Modern Maturity. A publication of AARP. Annual membership dues are $5.00 which include a subscription to *Modern Maturity* and the AARP news publication.

New Choices (formerly *50 Plus*). Write or call: *New Choices*, 850 Third Avenue, New York, New York 10022 (212-

715-2785). Subscription is $15.00 per year. Four booklets available from *New Choices: Finding the Right Place for Your Retirement; Planning Your Tomorrow Kit; Sixty-five Mistakes to Avoid in Retirement; Living Alone After Fifty.*

NATIONAL ORGANIZATIONS

AARP Fulfillment, P.O. Box 2240, Long Beach, California 90801. Offers members life, health, and auto insurance, reduced prescription and nonprescription drug prices, a nursing home, about five hundred local chapters. Operates Widowed Persons Service, which is a support group for widowed older persons. Also offers members a large variety of publications.

Administration on Aging, U.S. Department of Health and Human Services, Washington, D.C. 20201. Various publications.

American Association of Retired Persons (AARP), 1909 K Street, N.W., Washington, D.C. 20049.

National Association of Mature People, 2212 Northwest 50th Street, P.O. Box 26792, Oklahoma City, Oklahoma 73126. Educational material, prescription drug service, financial guidance.

National Council of Senior Citizens, 925 Fifteenth Street, N.W., Washington, D.C. 20005. Sponsors workshops and leadership training. Publishes *Senior Citizens News.*

Older Women's League (OWL), 1325 G Street, N.W., Lower Level B, Washington, D.C. 20005. Interests of older women, speakers' bureau, educational materials, publications.

NURSING HOMES

American Association of Homes for the Aging, 1129 20th Street, Washington, D.C. 20036 (202-296-5960).

American Health Care Association, 1201 L Street, N.W., Washington, D.C. 20005. For a brochure on choosing a nursing home, send a self-addressed stamped envelope.

American Nursing Home Association, 1101 Seventeenth Street, N.W., Washington, D.C. 20036. Object is to upgrade standards in nursing homes. Various publications.

Caring for the Aged, by C. Clyde Jones. Chicago: Nelson-Hall Publishers, 1982. An appraisal of nursing homes and alternatives.

Directory of Nursing Homes. Sam Mongeau. Phoenix: The Oryx Press, 1984. A state-by-state listing of facilities and services.

How to Choose a Nursing Home: A Shopping and Rating Guide. Available from Citizens for Better Care, 960 East Jefferson Avenue, Detroit, Michigan 48207.

How to Select a Nursing Home. Consumer Information Service, National Senior Citizens Education and Research Center, Inc., 925 Fifteenth Street, N.W., Washington, D.C. 20005.

U.S. Department of Health and Human Services, Health Care Financing Administration, Division of Long-Term Care, Baltimore, Maryland 21207. Write for free booklet on nursing homes, *Nursing Home Care*, HCFA77-24902.

When Love Gets Tough: The Nursing Home Decision, by Doug Manning. Hereford, Texas: In-Sight Books, 1983.

PEN PALS

International Pen Friends. For information write: Leslie Fox, Regional Representative, International Pen Friends, P.O. Box 290065, Homecrest Station, Brooklyn, New York 11229-0001. They have over 190,000 members in more than 153 countries. They will put you in touch with pen pals around the world, paying close attention to hobbies and special interests. Special attention is given to age groups. Publishes a magazine for members. Admission fee is low.

PETS

Homeless Pets for the Elderly Program. For information write: Purina Pets for People Program, Checkerboard Square 6T, Saint Louis, Missouri 63164.

RETIREMENT

Advertising Standards, Department RC, 3200 East Carson Street, Lakewood, California 90712. Write for more information on retirement communities.

American Association of Retired Persons. For a list of retirement communities (and other options) write, AARP, National Gerontology Resource Center, 1909 K Street, N.W., Washington, D.C. 20049.

Elderhostel organizes affordable, short-term learning programs at educational institutions throughout the United States, Canada, and more than thirty-five countries overseas. For free catalog and course offerings write: Elder-

hostel, Suite 400, 80 Boyleston Street, Boston, Massachusetts 02116.

Guide to Planning Your Retirement. Write for free booklet: AARP Worker Equity Department, 1909 K Street, N.W., Washington, D.C. 20049.

The Reality of Retirement, by Jules Willing. New York: William Morrow & Co., Inc., 1981.

Retirement: Coping with Emotional Upheavals, by Leland and Martha Bradford. Chicago: Nelson-Hall Publishers, 1979.

Sunbelt Retirement: Complete State-by-State Guide, by Peter Dickinson; AARP books/Scott, Foresman.

SAFETY

55-ALIVE Program. Offered all over the country by volunteer teachers and sponsored by AARP. For $7.00 and eight hours of time, the elderly will learn how to cope with the aging process and also be safer, better drivers.

The Home Safety Checklist: Safety for Older Consumers. Free. Organized by rooms in the home, can help identify possible safety problems and also provides suggestions for correction. Write or call: U.S. Consumer Product Safety Commission, Washington, D.C. 20207 (800-638-2772).

The Product Safety Book. $5.95 plus $1.00 shipping. A helpful book listing product hazards in your home; an encyclopedia of over five hundred products, from bathtubs to cordless phones, from mobile homes to tomato soup and antacids. Write: Consumer Federation of America, 1424 Sixteenth Street, N.W., Washington, D.C. 20036.

VOLUNTEER OPPORTUNITIES

Foster Grandparents Program, ACTION, The National Volunteer Agency, 1100 Vermont Avenue, N.W., Washington, D.C. 20525. (202-634-9349). A federal program that recruits men and women age sixty and over to work with children on 245 projects throughout the United States.

Intergenerational Clearinghouse Newsletter. Published by Retired Senior Volunteers Program of Dane County, Inc., Suite 210, 517 North Segoe Road, Madison, Wisconsin 53705 (608-238-RSVP). Contains information on new projects and updates on existing ones.

National School Volunteer Program, Suite 200, 601 Wythe Street, Alexandria, Virginia 22314 (800-992-6787). As part of the National Association of Partners in Education, it coordinates school volunteers and business people with schools in their area.

SCORE (Service Corps of Retired Executives) is sponsored by the U.S. Small Business Administration and comprises thirteen thousand volunteers, including retired business owners, executives, corporate leaders, accountants, lawyers, military officers, and other professionals. Members of SCORE give advice on fledgling businesses struggling to make it or having problems. The advice is confidential and free. SCORE has over six hundred offices in all fifty states and also on Guam, Puerto Rico, and the Virgin Islands. If you are a successful, retired business or professional person, SCORE wants to talk to you. You are not paid. Your compensation is the satisfaction derived from keeping active, counseling others, and being useful. Any travel expenses will be paid by SCORE. For more information and to locate the SCORE office nearest you, write or call; National SCORE Office, Suite 901, 655 Fifteenth Street, N.W., Washington, D.C. 20005 (202-653-6279).

TLC (Teaching, Learning Communities) Mentors Program, New Age, Inc., 1212 Roosevelt Road, Ann Arbor, Michigan 48014 (313-994-4715). Recruits older people to serve as mentors to junior high school students who are in danger of dropping out.

MISCELLANEOUS

Domestic Mistreatment of the Elderly. Booklet. Write: Criminal Justice Services, AARP Program Department, 1909 K Street, N.W., Washington, D.C. 20049.

The Gadget Book, edited by Dennis R. LaBuda. Ingenious devices for easier living. Lists hundreds of devices designed for the elderly. A "rocker" knife for cutting food with one hand, "reacher" tongs, and so on.

Mature Wisdom, Hanover, Pennsylvania 17333-0028 (800-621-5800). Free catalog of fashions, health and beauty aids, furniture, appliances, and so forth, geared toward the elderly.

Sears, Roebuck & Company Home Health Care Specialog. Ask for this catalog at your nearest Sears store.

Able-Data, National Rehabilitation Center, Washington, D.C. Special devices can be purchased for those with limited mobility. (800-346-2742).

The Ultimate Listening Source—a catalog of devices that can improve everyday life. To receive this catalog call (201) 347-7662.